P · O · C · K · E · T · S
TREES

P·O·C·K·E·T·S
TREES

Written by
THERESA GREENAWAY

APPLES

WHITE OAK ACORN

RED MAPLE LEAF

Reader's Digest

A DORLING KINDERSLEY BOOK

Project editor Fiona Robertson
Art editors Jane Tetzlaff
Clair Watson
Senior editor Susan McKeever
Senior art editor Helen Senior
Designer Alexandra Brown
Picture research Becky Halls
Anna Lord
Production Louise Barratt

First published in Australia in 1995 by
Reader's Digest (Australia) Pty Limited
26-32 Waterloo Street, Surry Hills, NSW 2010

Copyright © Dorling Kindersley Ltd., London

All rights reserved. Unauthorised reproduction, whether in whole or
in part, or in any manner, whether mechanical, electric or otherwise,
except as permitted under the Copyright Act or by the written
permission of the publisher, is prohibited.

The National Library of Australia Cataloguing-in-Publication data

Greenway, Theresa, 1947-
Trees.

Includes index.
ISBN 0 86438 813 6.
ISBN 0 86438 691 5 (series).

1. Trees. 2. Forest ecology. I. Title. (Series : Pockets).

582.16

Colour reproduction by Colourscan, Singapore
Printed and bound in Italy by L.E.G.O.

Contents

How to use this book 8

INTRODUCTION TO TREES 10
What is a tree? 12
Anatomy of a tree 20
How trees grow 38
Trees of the world 46

NORTHERN CONIFEROUS FORESTS 48
The habitat 50
The far north 52
Paper and timber 54
Pacific forests 56

TEMPERATE FORESTS 58
The habitat 60
North America 62
The southern states 64
Europe 66

By the river 68
Wetlands 70
Hedges 72
Central Europe 74
The Balkans 76
The Middle East 78
Fruits and nuts 80
Northern China 82
Central China 84
Southern China 86
Japan 88

TROPICAL FORESTS 92
The habitat 94
America 96
Tropical products 98
Tropical Africa 100
Tropical Asia 102
Mist forests 104
Australia 106

MIXED EVERGREEN FORESTS 108
The habitat 110
South-east Australia 112
New Zealand 114
California 116

South America 118
Mediterranean 120

MOUNTAIN FORESTS 124
The habitat 126
Rocky Mountains 128
The Himalayas 130

REFERENCE SECTION 134
Studying trees 136
Watching trees grow 138
Threats to trees 140
Tree classification 142

Glossary 148
Latin name index 152
Index 155
Resources 159

How to use this book

These pages show you how to use *Pockets: Trees*. The book is divided into several sections. The main section consists of information on trees from different habitats. There is also an introductory section at the front, and a reference section at the back. Each new section begins with a picture page and a guide to the contents of that section.

HABITATS
The trees in the book are arranged into habitats. In each habitat section, you will find information on the habitat, and examples of the types of tree that can be found growing there.

CORNER CODING
Corners of habitat pages are colour coded to remind you which habitat section you are in.

- NORTHERN CONIFEROUS FORESTS
- TEMPERATE FORESTS
- TROPICAL FORESTS
- MIXED EVERGREEN FORESTS
- MOUNTAIN FORESTS

HEADING
This describes the subject of the page. This page is about California. If a subject continues over several pages, the same heading applies.

INTRODUCTION
This provides a clear overview of the subject. After reading this, you should have an idea of what the following pages are about.

CAPTIONS AND ANNOTATIONS
Each illustration has a caption. Annotations, in *italics*, point out features of an illustration and usually have leader lines.

8

RUNNING HEADS
These remind you which section you are in. The top of the left-hand page gives the section name. The right-hand page gives the subject. This page on California is in the Mixed Evergreen Forests section.

FACT BOXES
Many pages have fact boxes (not shown here). These contain at-a-glance information about the subject, such as the tallest tree or the oldest tree to be found in that area.

SHAPE INDICATORS
Where part of a tree is shown, a silhouette of the whole tree is next to the picture to give an indication of the tree's shape.

REFERENCE SECTION
The reference section pages are yellow and appear at the back of the book. On these pages, you will find useful facts and figures. There is also advice on how to plant and grow your own trees, and on how to identify different species.

LABELS
For extra clarity, some pictures have labels. The labels may identify a picture when it is not obvious from the text what it is, or they may give extra information about the subject.

INDEX
There are two indexes at the back of the book – a subject index, and a Latin name index. The subject index lists every subject alphabetically. The Latin name index lists the Latin names of all the trees in the book.

INTRODUCTION TO TREES

WHAT IS A TREE? 12
ANATOMY OF A TREE 20
HOW TREES GROW 38
TREES OF THE WORLD 46

INTRODUCTION

WHAT IS A TREE?

A TREE IS A WOODY PLANT that grows at least 5 m (16 ft) tall. It has a single trunk that supports a leafy crown of branches above the ground. Trees can live for a hundred years or longer. A woody plant with branches at ground level is called a shrub.

EARLY TREES
Tall, woody, tree-like plants have covered the Earth's surface for over 359 million years. Lepidodendron, one of the earliest trees, flourished during the Carboniferous period. It was over 30 m (100 ft) tall, but was more closely related to ferns than to today's trees.

TREE TYPES
There are three main groups of tree. Broadleaved trees, which are often deciduous, are the most numerous and widespread. Conifers are almost all evergreen, and palm trees have a distinctive crown.

BROADLEAVED TREE   CONIFER   PALM TREE

Branch

Leaves

WHAT IS A TREE?

Crown

HARDY TREES
In dry desert areas, only specially adapted trees can survive the lack of moisture. The acacia, for example, sheds its leaves during the dry season to save water.

Stem acts as leaves

COMMON OAK

A LEAFLESS "TREE"
At 12 m (40 ft) high, the saguaro cactus is as tall as many trees. However, it has no leaves, and instead of a woody trunk, it has a tough stem that stores water.

Trunk

A TYPICAL TREE
Trees will grow wherever there is enough light, warmth, and moisture. However, even in favourable conditions and rich soil, a species such as an oak (shown here) can take many years to grow into a mature tree.

13

Broadleaved trees

Trees with broad, flat leaves belong to a group of plants called angiosperms, or "vessel seeds". They all produce flowers, and their seeds develop in a vessel, called a fruit. Broadleaved trees are found in tropical and temperate climates. In temperate climates, most are deciduous and shed their leaves in autumn.

BIRD CHERRY
Broadleaved trees often have colourful, scented flowers, which attract birds and insects. The bird cherry has small white flowers arranged in spikes.

HOLLY
Unlike most broadleaved trees in temperate regions, the holly does not shed its leaves in autumn.

TUPELO
Broadleaved trees, such as this tupelo, often have thin, flat leaves that are easily damaged by strong winds, frost, and snow. The leaves are therefore shed in autumn.

These splendid autumn colours are caused by chemical changes inside the leaves.

BEECH LEAF
Broadleaves, such as this beech, have a distinctive network of veins that connects to a central midrib. The veins transport food and water around the leaf.

WHAT IS A TREE?

ASH TREE
This typical broadleaved tree has a wide spreading crown supported by a sturdy trunk. Below the ground, criss-crossing roots anchor the ash to the ground. Tiny branchlets at the end of each branch divide further into a mass of fine twigs.

EUROPEAN ASH

Smooth, yellowish-grey twigs and branches

BROADLEAF FACTS
- The tallest broadleaved tree is the Australian mountain ash, which can reach 107 m (350 ft).
- Many broadleaved trees live for 100-300 years; oak trees, for example, can reach 500 years old.

ASH FRUITS
Each ash "key" is a fruit that contains a seed. The seed is enclosed within a tough, leathery fruit wall that is shaped like a wing at one end.

15

INTRODUCTION

Conifer trees

Conifers belong to a group of plants called gymnosperms, which means "naked seed". Their seeds lie between the scales of female cones, and are never fully enclosed. Conifers are either trees or woody shrubs, and most are evergreen, which means the leaves remain on the tree all year round. Conifers grow all over the world, particularly in cold areas.

NORWAY SPRUCE
The Norway spruce has light brown cones. This conifer is often used as a Christmas tree.

CONIFER SHAPES
In many conifers, such as the cypress (right), the branches grow upwards to produce a flame shaped tree. Young pines are often cone shaped.

CYPRESS

MONTEREY PINE

A Monterey pine may lose its regular, conical shape as it matures.

CONIFER FACTS
- The oldest living trees on Earth are bristlecone pines from Arizona and Nevada, U.S.A., which are 5,000 years old.
- The largest tree is a wellingtonia, the General Sherman, at 83 m (273 ft) tall and 2,030 tonnes (tons).

WHAT IS A TREE?

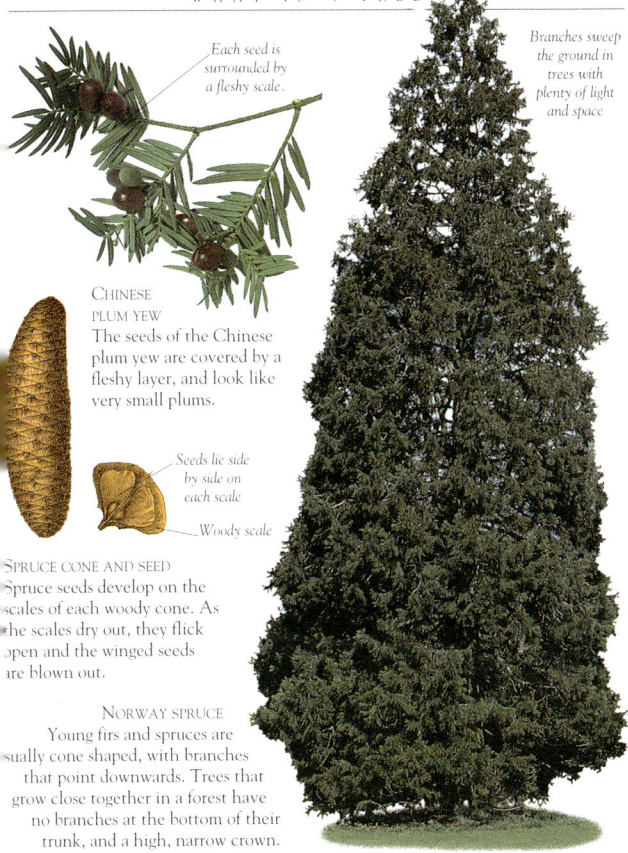

Each seed is surrounded by a fleshy scale.

Branches sweep the ground in trees with plenty of light and space

CHINESE PLUM YEW
The seeds of the Chinese plum yew are covered by a fleshy layer, and look like very small plums.

Seeds lie side by side on each scale

Woody scale

SPRUCE CONE AND SEED
Spruce seeds develop on the scales of each woody cone. As the scales dry out, they flick open and the winged seeds are blown out.

NORWAY SPRUCE
Young firs and spruces are usually cone shaped, with branches that point downwards. Trees that grow close together in a forest have no branches at the bottom of their trunk, and a high, narrow crown.

Palm trees

With their tall, bare trunks and huge crown of leaves, palm trees are easy to recognize. They flourish in warm, damp tropical regions – particularly Malaysia, Central America, and parts of the Amazon basin – but also grow on subtropical mountainsides and savannah grasslands. Palms are more closely related to grasses and lilies than to broadleaved trees. Unlike other trees, a palm tree trunk becomes only slightly thicker as the tree grows.

GERMINATING COCONUT

Young coconut leaf

DATE PALM

COCONUT PALM
The coconut is found on tropical coastlines throughout the world. Each fully grown coconut leaf is like a giant feather, 6 m (20 ft) long. Dried white coconut flesh, called copra, is used for food and to make soap and candles.

DATES

Single, fibrous stem with no branches

DATE PALM
Date palms grow best in hot, dry places with a good underground water supply, and have been cultivated in the Middle East and North Africa for centuries. Date palm fronds are pinnate – each feather-like leaf has two rows of leaflets. The dates grow in clusters of up to 1,500.

WHAT IS A TREE?

MALE CHUSAN PALM FLOWERS

Male flowers with anthers containing pollen

STORMY WEATHER
Palm trees have a tough but flexible trunk, made up of woody fibres. In a tropical cyclone, the trunk can bend and sway without snapping.

CHUSAN PALM
Each fan-shaped frond of the chusan palm is about 1 m (3 ft) across. The leaf blade is divided into stiff, narrow segments.

CHUSAN PALM FLOWERS
Yellow, sweetly scented chusan palm flowers form clusters in flowerheads up to 80 cm (30 in) long. Male and female flowers grow on separate trees.

Long, toothed stalk supports leaf blade

ANATOMY OF A TREE

A TREE IS MADE UP of many parts. Below the ground, the roots take up water and minerals from the soil. These pass up the trunk, which is protected by a layer of bark, into the leaves. Branches support the tree's leaves, flowers, and fruits.

BONSAI
A tree that has been "miniaturized" by confining its roots in a small container is called a bonsai.

The crown

A tree's crown is made up of twigs, branches, and leaves. The pattern of growth and the arrangement of twigs, branches and leaves differs from species to species. It is often possible to identify a tree simply by the shape of its crown.

EXPOSED TREES
Trees in exposed areas can be affected permanently by strong winds. Leaves and twigs facing the wind are killed, and the crown becomes extremely lopsided.

ANATOMY OF A TREE

POLLARDED WILLOW

SHAPED TREES
Trees that are pollarded have their branches cut off so that new shoots grow out from the top of the trunk, too high to be eaten by cattle or deer. Street trees may be pollarded, to prevent large branches hitting telephone wires or blocking light from buildings.

ROOKS
A tree's crown provides the ideal nesting place for many species of bird. Rooks build their twiggy nests close together, high in the tops of tall trees.

LEAFY CROWN
This tree has grown in an open area, with plenty of light and space to develop a full, leafy crown. In a dense, crowded forest, the same kind of tree has a taller trunk and a narrower crown, as the twigs reach towards the light.

INTRODUCTION

Broadleaves

A broadleaved tree has thin, flat leaves. The leaves are arranged on a tree to receive as much sunlight as possible. This is important because green leaves use the energy in sunlight to make all the food a tree needs to live and grow. A waterproof cuticle covers the leaf. On the underside, tiny pores called stomata allow gases to pass in and out of the leaf.

ALTERNATE   OPPOSITE

LEAF ARRANGEMENT
Broadleaves are arranged alternately along each twig, or in opposite pairs. The leaflets of compound leaves are also arranged in this way.

WINTER TWIGS AND BUDS
A crescent-shaped scar on a winter twig shows where a leaf has fallen. New buds form along the twig during the summer, but remain inactive until the next spring. Each bud contains tightly furled leaves, protected by tough bud scales.

INSIDE A BUD

TWIG FROM PEAR TREE

Single bud at tip of each twig

A large vein called the midrib runs down the centre of the leaf.

22

ANATOMY OF A TREE

Autumn leaves

Leaves contain a green pigment called chlorophyll which gives them their colour. In autumn, chlorophyll and other pigments in the leaf break down. These chemical changes cause the leaves to change colour.

The white oak has reddish-brown leaves in autumn.

WHITE OAK

ORIENTAL PLANE TREE

Yellow colour produced by pigments in the leaf

A typical broadleaf

Each leaf consists of a wide, flat blade, the lamina, that is supported by a leaf stalk, called the petiole. Within the lamina is a network of fine veins that transport water, minerals, and sugars around the leaf.

NORWAY MAPLE

Leaf variations

Simple leaves have a single leaf blade, which is called a lamina.

In compound leaves, the lamina is divided up into a number of leaflets.

A lobed leaf or leaflet is divided into segments that do not reach the midrib.

A leaf or leaflet edge may be toothed (jagged), or untoothed (smooth).

Conifer leaves

Nearly all conifers are evergreen. Their tough, spiky leaves can withstand harsh, wintry weather, and remain on the tree for two years or more. Conifer leaves come in a variety of shapes. Pines, larches, and cedars have needles; firs, yews, and some redwoods have flatter, strap-shaped leaves; and cypresses have scales.

MAIDENHAIR TREE

ENGRAVING OF A PINE NEEDLE

NORWAY SPRUCE

New needles

YOUNG SHOOT
Conifer buds open in late spring or early summer. In the Norway spruce (left), the young shoots and foliage are soft and light green, and look very different from the older, darker leaves.

Old needles

CONIFER LEAF
A typical conifer leaf has a narrow blade, called a lamina, that is dark and waxy. A single vein runs down the centre of the leaf. Like the trunk and roots, a conifer's leaves produce resin, which runs through tubes called ducts. Resin helps to prevent insects attacking the tree.

LEAF SHAPES
Strap-shaped leaves are smooth and glossy, with a leathery texture. Scale leaves are very tiny and packed closely together. Needles are narrow, often stiff, leaves that may be pointed.

STRAPS   NEEDLES   SCALES

LEAF ARRANGEMENT
Needles and strap-shaped leaves may be arranged in spirals, whorls, or rows. Pines have needles in bundles of two, three, or five. Scale leaves, such as on this Hinoki cypress, are in densely packed, opposite pairs.

ANATOMY OF A TREE

BUNDLES
The Austrian pine has long, dark green needles arranged in bundles of two. Each needle has a thick waxy outer layer, called a cuticle. This helps to prevent water loss.

Soft, flexible needles are shed in autumn.

LARCH

AUSTRIAN PINE

Sharp, pointed needles

HINOKI CYPRESS

SPIRALS AND WHORLS
Larch needles grow singly on new, long shoots, and are arranged spirally along the shoots. On older parts of the twigs, the needles grow in dense whorls on short shoots.

Flat sprays of scale-like leaves arranged in unequal pairs along the twig

CHINESE PLUM YEW

ROWS
The yellowish-green leaves of Chinese plum yew are arranged in two very regular rows along its twigs. These glossy, tapering leaves are between 4-9 cm (2-4 in) long.

The trunk

The round, woody stem of a tree is called the trunk. The trunk has to be strong enough to support the weight of the tree's branches, leaves, and fruits, and flexible enough to allow the tree to bend in the wind without snapping. The trunk also carries water, sugars, and nutrients to all parts of the tree. Woody cells have tough cellulose walls, which make the trunk and branches flexible. The cells also contain a chemical called lignin, which gives wood its rigidity.

LIVING ON THE TRUNK
In damp, temperate areas, trees such as this oak often have mosses growing around the base of the trunk, and ivy scrambling up to the crown. Bracket fungi indicate that wood-rotting fungi have infected the heart of the trunk. Birds such as woodpeckers peck holes in the bark to find insect larvae.

Bracket fungi

Ivy

MALE STAG BEETLE

STAG BEETLE
The larvae of the stag beetle hatch in dead tree stumps and rotting roots. The large, white larvae chew through wood for three years before turning into pupae.

ANATOMY OF A TREE

Bark protects the living tissues of the wood

TRUNK GROWTH
A trunk gets a little wider every year, but it can only grow longer from the tip of its leading shoot. Once a branch has forked away from the trunk, it too can only grow from its tip.

Heartwood
Cambium – region of growth
Medulla ray – carries nutrients inwards
Growth ring
Sapwood
Bark
Sapwood – living cells that conduct water
Heartwood – dead cells that give strength and support

WELLINGTONIA

CROSS-SECTION OF A TRUNK
Each year's growth appears on a trunk as an annual growth ring. A tree's age can be calculated by counting the rings. Wide rings show rapid growth, narrow rings indicate slower growth.

Annual growth ring

INTRODUCTION

Bark

Covering the trunk, branches, and twigs of a tree is a protective waterproof layer – the bark. Bark is thin and smooth when it is young, but may become thick and corky as the tree ages. It contains substances such as resins, which help to deter insect attack. The corky bark also prevents water loss from the trunk, and acts as an insulator.

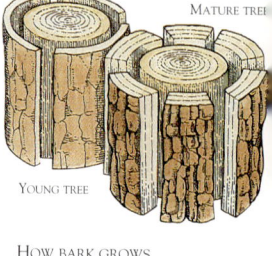

MATURE TREE

YOUNG TREE

BARK DESTROYER
The bark beetle can bore through bark to lay its eggs. The grubs make tunnels beneath the bark, chewing their way along.

BARK BEETLE

HOW BARK GROWS
Bark has to grow to keep pace with the expanding tree trunk, and to replace areas that have been damaged. A layer called the bark cambium forms a new layer of bark each year, which pushes the layer from the previous year outwards. The oldest bark forms the outer layers of the trunk.

Deep cracks and ridges

ANATOMY OF A TREE

TYPES OF BARK

Smooth bark: many young trees have smooth, thin bark dotted with pores called lenticels.

Plates: the bark of this tree has cracked as it ages into irregular areas called plates.

Thick bark: the outer layer of bark cracks into ridges as the trunk widens.

Vertically peeling: some bark peels off in vertical strips to reveal younger layers below.

Horizontally peeling: this bark peels off the trunk in horizontal bands.

Flaking bark: bark that flakes off in uneven patches makes the trunk rough.

TROPICAL AND TEMPERATE BARK

Tropical rainforest trees usually have thin bark because the temperature is warm all year. Temperate trees have thicker bark to protect them from temperature extremes. The ash (left) is a temperate tree that has distinctive, thick bark.

Amber is fossilized resin that oozed from wounds in the bark of conifers millions of years ago.

Amber is often used to make jewellery.

FOSSILIZED AMBER

Roots

A tree's roots have two main tasks. They anchor the tree firmly in the ground, and they absorb water and dissolved minerals from the soil. Most roots grow outwards through the soil, rather than downwards, and can reach distances underground that equal the height of the tree.

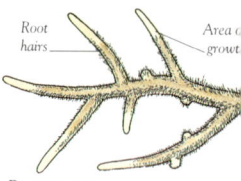

ROOT HAIRS
Tiny, hair-like outgrowths of the cells just behind the root tips are called root hairs. All root hairs die in autumn and new ones grow in spring.

SWAMP CYPRESS
Many trees cannot survive in water-logged soil because it is low in oxygen. However, mangroves and swamp cypresses have special breathing roots, called pneumatophores, that stick up above the surface. The oxygen they absorb passes around the root system.

A TYPICAL ROOT
Roots lengthen only at their tips. They divide repeatedly, forming fine rootlets that spread through the soil, pushing into cracks between rocks or stones. As they grow older, roots become woody and a little thicker.

ROOTS AND FUNGI
Many types of fungi get their food by spreading through the roots of trees such as birches or pines. The fly agaric (right) wraps itself around birch roots as it grows. The tree benefits because the fungus supplies it with scarce soil nutrients.

INTRODUCTION

Flowers

A flower's main function is to bring about pollination so that seeds can be formed for reproduction. Flowers contain a tree's male and female reproductive parts – the stamens and the carpels. Showy, often scented petals attract pollinators. Sepals protect the flower bud, and are arranged with petals, stamens, and carpels in whorl

FLOWERING DOGWOOD
These large pink "petals" are in fact coloured leaves called bracts. The real petals are small and green, and form clusters of flowers that nestle in the centre of the bracts.

Young leaves appear as the tree flowers.

Tiny flowers grow in clusters.

REDBUD
Each flower on the redbud tree has five differently shaped petals. The lowest petal is called the keel, and forms an insect's landing pad. The side petals, called wings, and the top petal, or standard, guide the insect in towards the nectar. The flowers grow on thin stalks in clusters of two to eight.

REDBUD

ANATOMY OF A TREE

CALIFORNIAN BUCKEYE
A cluster of flowers is called an inflorescence. The Californian buckeye can have inflorescences up to 20 cm (8 in) long. Each flower has four petals and long, protruding stamens.

BIRCH CATKIN
Numerous male flowers are arranged in yellow catkins that hang down below the twigs. Female flowers are in separate, upright catkins.

Male and female flowers growing on the same tree.

MAGNOLIA DAWSONIANA

MAGNOLIA
In a magnolia flower, the stamens and carpels are arranged spirally around a central spike.

Sepals and petals look the same and are called tepals.

STAMEN AND CARPEL
The stamen has a thin stalk, the filament, and a small sac, the anther. The ovary, the stigma, and the style make up the carpel. These parts can be located on the same flower or on separate flowers.

APPLE TREE IN BLOSSOM

INTRODUCTION

Fruits and seeds

Once a flower has been pollinated, its petals fall and the fruit begins to grow. The fruit contains and protects the flower's seeds. Seeds are the reproductive part of a tree, and are shed when the fruit is ripe. If the tree uses animals to spread its seeds, the fruit may be sweet and juicy. If the seeds are scattered by the wind, the fruit is often light and dry. Each seed contains an embryo that will grow into a new tree. One or more seed leaves, called cotyledons, store the food needed to fuel the seed's growth.

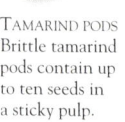

TAMARIND PODS
Brittle tamarind pods contain up to ten seeds in a sticky pulp.

LEMON FRUIT AND SEEDS

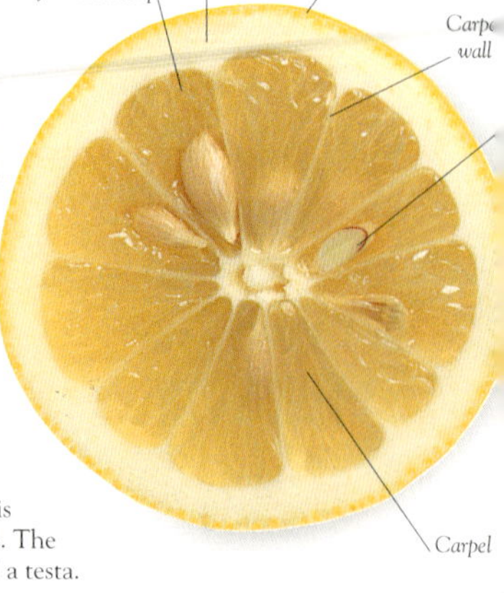

Embryo
Cotyledon (seed leaf)
Endocarp
Mesocarp
Epicarp
Carpel wall

Testa (seed coat)

CITRUS FRUITS
Fruits have an outer skin, the epicarp; a middle layer, the mesocarp; and an inner endocarp. Citrus fruits, such as the lemon, are a kind of berry. They are made up of several segments. The juicy flesh is the endocarp and contains the seeds. The seeds have a woody seed coat, called a testa.

Carpel

3 4

APPLES

These cultivated apples are much larger and sweeter than wild apples. Each one is a "false" fruit, called a pome. The thick layer of sweet, edible flesh is actually the swollen tip of the flower stalk, called the receptacle. The "true" fruit is the apple core, which contains leathery-skinned apple pips. These are the seeds.

Sweet, fleshy apple

THE "WORCESTER PEARMAIN", A MODERN VARIETY

SWEET CHESTNUT

The fruit of the sweet chestnut is a shiny brown nut. The hard fruit wall, called the pericarp, protects the soft seed inside. A spiky shell encloses the nuts and splits to release them when they are ripe.

SYCAMORE SEED

The winged fruit of the sycamore is split into two halves. Each half contains a seed protected by a tough fruit wall. Inside the seed are two cotyledons and a tiny embryo.

Remains of sepal
Seed
Pedicel (flower stalk)
Remains of stigma and style
Testa (seed coat)
Pericarp (fruit wall, flattened to form wing)

35

Cones

A cone is made up of overlapping scales, arranged spirally around a central spike. Male cones produce pollen, which blows on the wind to female cones. Once the pollen is shed, the male cone falls. Seeds develop within the female cone, which can remain on the tree for three years or longer.

Tightly overlapping scales

Disintegrating cone

Seeds attached to scale

CEDAR CONES
Smooth, egg-shaped cedar cones stand upright on the tops of the twigs. They gradually disintegrate when they are ripe.

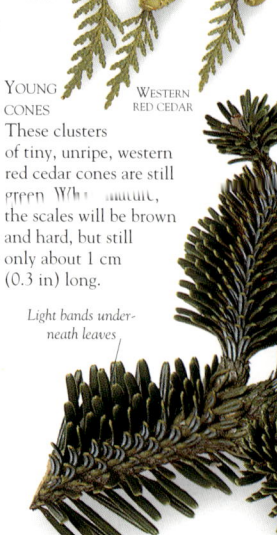

YOUNG CONES

WESTERN RED CEDAR

These clusters of tiny, unripe, western red cedar cones are still green. When mature, the scales will be brown and hard, but still only about 1 cm (0.3 in) long.

Light bands underneath leaves

YOUNG MALE AND FEMALE CONES
Male cones produce pollen from sacs on the lower surface of each scale. Female cones contain the female sex cells, called ovules, which lie on the scales.

Scale on female cone bears ovule, then seed

MALE CONE   FEMALE CONE

3 6

ANATOMY OF A TREE

DOUGLAS FIR CONE

HANGING CONES
Young, green Douglas fir cones hang down below the branches. They have a three-pronged bract between each scale.

Three-pronged bract

Closed cone

Tiny bract

FORREST'S FIR

Scales parted

OPEN SUGAR PINE CONE

FIR CONES
All true firs have upright cones, perched high up on the branches like fat candles. Unlike spruce and pine cones, which fall to the ground intact, fir cones break up while they are still on the tree.

OPEN CONE
Cones only open in hot, dry weather, when their winged seeds are shaken out. The sugar pine belongs to a group of pines that produce long, cylindrical cones. Sugar pine cones can be up to 40 cm (16 in) long.

How trees grow

TREES TRAP THE ENERGY in sunlight to produce sugars. These sugars are the building blocks of the substances needed to make the tree's roots, trunk, leaves, flowers, and fruits. The sugars also provide the tree with the energy to grow and produce seeds.

Growth and nutrition

Mineral nutrients are essential to a tree's growth. They help to make cell walls, proteins, and chlorophyll, the pigment needed for photosynthesis. Minerals are dissolved in soil moisture, and are absorbed by the root hairs.

Roots

A network of spreading roots anchors the tree in the ground.

The woody trunk grows a little thicker each year.

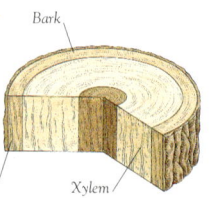

Bark

Phloem

Xylem

XYLEM AND PHLOEM
Woody-walled, non-living xylem cells carry water and minerals upwards from a tree's roots. A thin layer of living phloem cells just below the bark transports sugars from the leaves to all other parts of the tree.

MAKING FOOD

Green plants use the Sun's energy to make sugars from carbon dioxide and water. This process is called photosynthesis. It can only occur if a pigment called chlorophyll is present.

Sugars *Sunlight* *Water* *Carbon dioxide* *Oxygen*

TREE GROWTH

At the tip of every twig there is a group of specialized cells. These cells divide to make the twig longer, which in turn increases the height of the tree and the width of its crown. Cells in the cambium also divide to make the trunk, roots, and branches thicker.

Flower bud

Apical bud

Wood cells have walls reinforced with a substance called lignin.

TREE MALLOW

REDWOOD

A tree's trunk acts like a plumbing system. Water is drawn upwards in a column from the roots through the trunk to the leaves. In very tall trees, such as redwoods, the column of water can be 100 m (330 ft) high.

Pollination

Before seeds can develop, pollen must be transferred from the male parts of a flower to the female parts. This process is called pollination. Each pollen grain contains male sex cells, which, after pollination, fertilize the female sex cells in an ovule. Broadleaved trees have ovules enclosed within an ovary. In coniferous trees, the ovules lie on cone scales. Pollination can occur within the same flower, or between flowers on different plants.

SCOTS PINE
Large amounts of dry, dusty pollen are carried by the wind from the male cones to the female cones. Pine pollen has two tiny air sacs on each grain. These help to make it very light.

HAZEL CATKINS
The flowers of many wind-pollinated broadleaved trees develop in long catkins. The flowers open before the leaves so that the pollen can drift among the bare twigs. The flowers do not need to attract insects, and have no scent or nectar.

TULIP TREE
Some trees have large, brightly coloured petals and a sugary liquid called nectar to attract insects. The tulip tree has greenish-yellow petals and sticky pollen that clings to visiting insects.

Sepals

Petal

Central spike of female carpels

TULIP TREE BLOSSOM

HUMMINGBIRDS
The hummingbird's long, tube-like beak allows it to drink nectar from deep inside trumpet-shaped flowers. As it feeds, pollen sticks to feathers on its head and may be brushed off onto the next flower the bird visits.

A bee scrapes pollen off its body into pollen baskets on its hind legs.

BUSY BEES
Bees are important pollinators because they fly between flowers, drinking nectar and spreading pollen. They also take nectar and pollen back to their hives. Nectar is turned into honey and stored in the honeycomb. This, together with the pollen, provides food for the hive.

Large, scented petals attract pollinators

WILD CRAB APPLE BLOSSOM

Seed dispersal

A seed needs light, water, and space to grow, and must be spread, or dispersed, away from the parent tree. Trees rely mostly on animals, birds, or the wind to scatter their seeds. Wind-dispersed seeds may have tiny sails to help them drift away. Animal-dispersed seeds are often in tasty fruits, or in hooked fruits that cling to an animal's fur.

COMMON FIG

SCATTERED SEEDS
Birds and monkeys eat sweet, fleshy figs. Small seeds inside the figs pass through their bodies unharmed and are left behind in their droppings. This helps to disperse the seeds.

WATER DISPERSAL
Each coconut seed is protected by a hard, woody shell and a fibrous husk, which is waterproof. Coconuts can float, and will sprout and grow if they are washed up on a warm, sandy shore.

HIDDEN STORES
Dry seeds or nuts, such as acorns, are eaten by birds and animals such as jays and squirrels. Many nut eaters bury their food and then forget about it. The seeds survive and often begin to grow in the spring.

GREY SQUIRREL

Squirrels forage for nuts on the forest floor.

LABURNUM FRUITS

Some seeds, such as those on the laburnum, develop inside long hanging pods. As the seed ripens, the pod dries out. It eventually splits along two sides, flicking the hard, dry seeds away from the parent plant.

Seeds are scattered as pod splits open.

HAWTHORN FRUITS

Birds feast on bright red hawthorn berries during the autumn and winter. The fruits are swallowed whole. The flesh is digested and the hard, woody-walled seeds pass out in the bird's droppings.

Bright red, juicy hawthorn berries

Germination

The growth of seeds into seedlings is called germination. Trees may produce thousands and thousands of seeds in a single year. Many of these are eaten by animals, or land somewhere they cannot grow. Only a few seeds survive the first years and even fewer reach maturity. Tree seeds often go through a period of inactivity called dormancy during the winter. This avoids the risk of seedlings being killed by frost.

BEECH LEAF AND FRUIT

OAK SEEDLING
A germinating seedling uses food stored in thick, fleshy seed leaves, called cotyledons. This oak seedling is showing hypogeal germination – the cotyledons remain below the ground as the shoot grows upwards.

Stem

Cotyledons remain below ground

Root

1 GERMINATION BEGINS
The woody case of a beech nut splits to release the seeds. When germination begins, the seeds absorb water and swell. The tiny embryo uses food stored in the cotyledons to start growing.

Seed case splits into four parts

Three-sided seed attached to case

Seed case

Stem

2 BEECH SEEDLING
The root pushes deeper into the soil, and rootlets branch out from it. Beech seeds show epigeal germination – a stem carries the cotyledons above the soil surface, still partly encased in the seed coat.

Rootlets

Main root

3 GROWING UP

Fourteen days after germination, the cotyledons are well above the soil, but are still folded. They begin to unfold and turn green, which allows them to make food by photosynthesis. The seed coat is pushed off. The new shoot is visible as a tiny green bud between the two cotyledons.

True leaves with veins as in an adult tree

4 BURSTING INTO LEAF

The seed is now one month old and developing a complex root system. The first pair of true leaves appears, which look just like an adult tree. As more leaves open, the seed leaves wither and fall, and the slender stem becomes woody.

Seed case forced off by seed leaves

Emerging seed leaves will begin to make food

Stem

Seed case

Main root

Rootlets

Seed leaves will wither at end of first year

Stem

Main root

Rootlets

FULLY GROWN BEECH
After two years, a beech seedling is still only a few centimetres (just over an inch) tall. It will take over 50 years to develop the sturdy trunk and spreading crown of the mature tree.

INTRODUCTION

TREES OF THE WORLD

TREES WILL GROW wherever there is enough rainfall and the summers are warm enough. Where the conditions are right, many trees will grow close together in woods and forests. In other places, where it is too dry for forests to survive, small numbers of trees will flourish along the banks of rivers or lakes.

TEMPERATE FORESTS
Places with mild summers, cold winters, and moderate rainfall all year long have temperate forests. They contain mostly broadleaved trees.

MOUNTAIN FORESTS
With an increase in altitude, the climate becomes cooler and harsher. The forests on mountain slopes are mostly coniferous. The height above which it is too cold for trees to grow is called the tree line.

NORTHERN CONIFEROUS FOREST
Long, harsh winters and brief summers characterize these forests. To the north is the Arctic, where it is too cold for trees to grow. Coastal regions have plenty of rain, but farther inland it is drier.

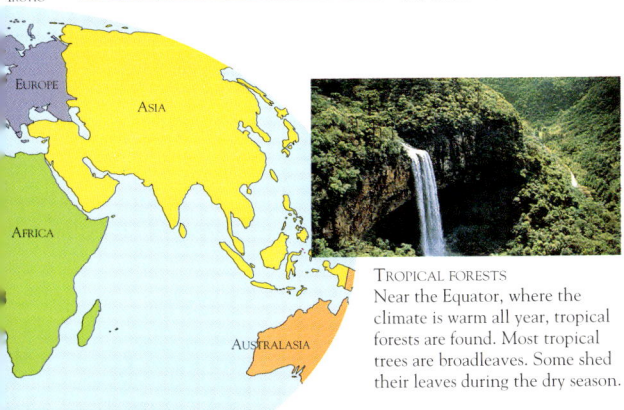

TROPICAL FORESTS
Near the Equator, where the climate is warm all year, tropical forests are found. Most tropical trees are broadleaves. Some shed their leaves during the dry season.

MIXED EVERGREEN FORESTS
Forests that contain conifers and evergreen broadleaved trees grow in places with mild, wet winters and hot, dry summers. They also occur in areas that are wet all year round, with frost-free winters and mild summers.

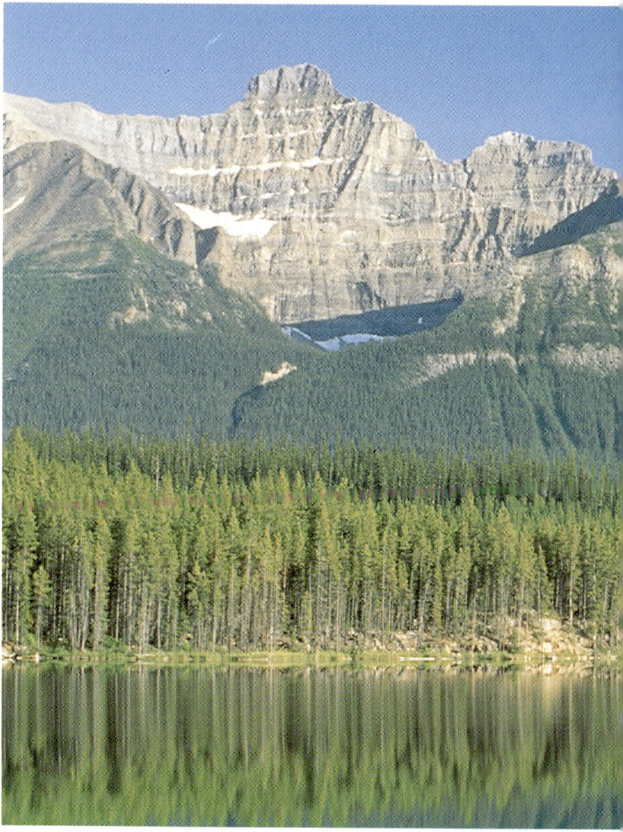

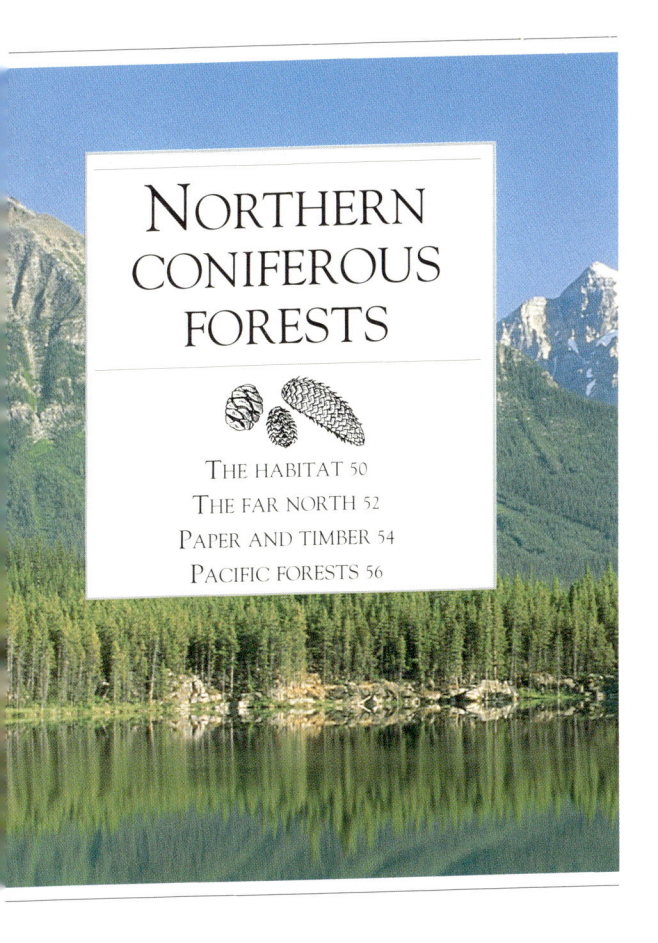

Northern Coniferous Forests

The habitat 50
The far north 52
Paper and timber 54
Pacific forests 56

NORTHERN CONIFEROUS FORESTS

NORWAY SPRUCE

THE HABITAT

THE NORTHERN CONIFEROUS forest forms a belt across North America, northern Europe, and northern Asia. It is known as the boreal forest after Boreas, Greek god of the North Wind. Long, harsh winters and short summers mean that trees in these forests have a short growing season. Farther north, the Arctic tundra is too cold for trees to grow.

CONIFEROUS FOREST
Conifers are best adapted to survive in the harsh conditions of the northern winter. Their evergreen leaves allow them to photosynthesize whenever there is enough light.

HABITAT FACTS

• There are 5 million sq km (2 million sq miles) of boreal forest.

• "Taiga" is the Russian word for boreal forest.

• In the deepest parts of the boreal forest, only mosses and lichens grow on the acidic peaty soil of the forest floor.

WOLF
The wildernesses of the boreal forest are home to the grey wolf. Wolves are carnivores, preying on many animals, including deer.

THE HABITAT

GROUND BEETLES
On the forest floor, ground beetles scuttle over fallen conifer needles, preying on other insects.

FALLEN NEEDLES
Falling pine needles from trees such as the western hemlock build up on the forest floor. The needles break down slowly in the cool climate to form a type of acid soil called peat.

WESTERN HEMLOCK

SCOTS PINE

Bark of upper part of tree is orange

A SHADY PLACE
The large, flat-topped crowns of trees such as the Scots pine block light from the forest floor, making it dark and gloomy. A few acid-loving grasses and shrubs will grow in the gaps between the trees.

THE FAR NORTH

NORTHERN FORESTS are a patchwork of different environments. White spruce grow on drier soils, black spruce survive in waterlogged areas, and larches tolerate the harsh regions near the Arctic Circle. Hardy broadleaved trees grow near rivers and lakes.

WHITE SPRUCE

THE TREE OF LIFE
In Norse mythology, a mighty ash tree called Yggdrasil links the Earth with heaven and hell. Yggdrasil is the tree of life.

SWEDISH SCENE
Central Sweden is an area of lakes, rivers, and mountains. Coniferous forests and plantations cover much of the land.

Mountainside trees grow on thin, rocky soils.

THE FAR NORTH

PAPER BIRCH
This is one of the few broadleaved trees of the North American boreal forest. Paper birch grows on moist, sandy soils. Its smooth, chalky-white bark was once used by Native Americans to make their canoes.

Slender, needle leaves

Leaves turn yellow and orange in autumn.

Egg-shaped, reddish-brown hanging cones

BLACK SPRUCE
This dark spruce is common throughout the boreal forest of North America. It grows on wet, peaty soil in boggy areas. Roots sprout where the lower branches touch the ground, and a new tree will develop.

Lakeside trees need roots that can tolerate waterlogged soils.

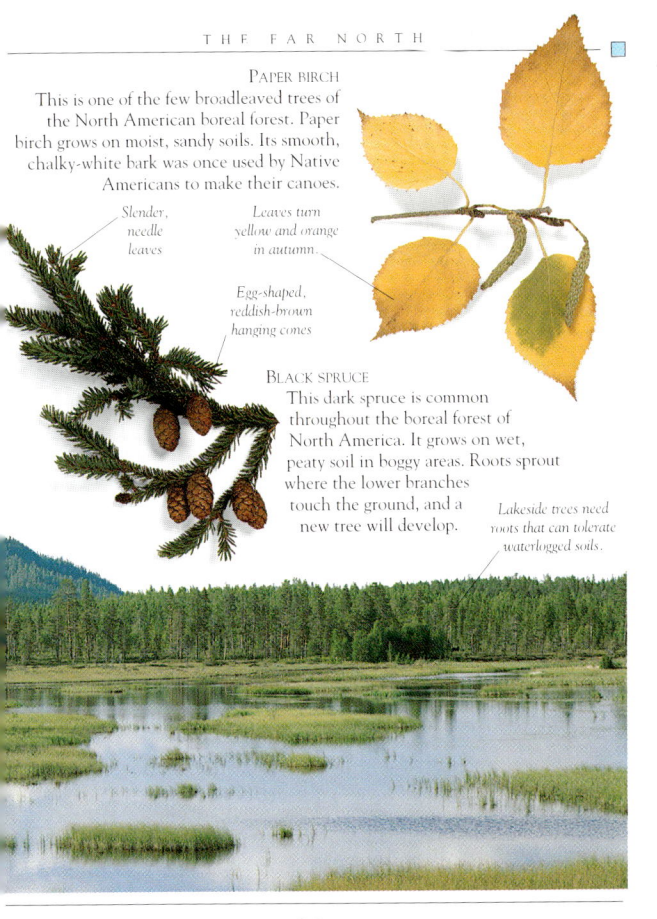

NORTHERN CONIFEROUS FORESTS

PAPER AND TIMBER

WOOD IS A MAJOR world resource – about 3,000 million tonnes (tons) are used for different purposes every year. Natural forests are still exploited for timber, but much of the wood that is harvested, especially to make paper, comes from trees grown in plantations.

ENGRAVING OF A WOOD TURNER

WOOD TO PAPER
Paper is made in a factory called a paper mill. Pale-coloured, low-grade wood is ideal for paper. The wood is turned into a pulp, which is pressed and rolled into paper.

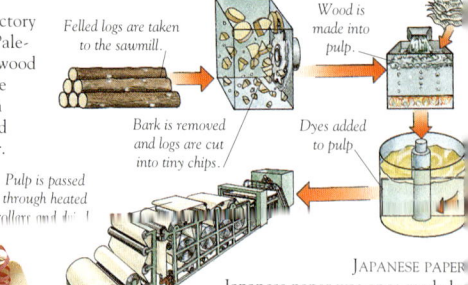

Felled logs are taken to the sawmill.

Bark is removed and logs are cut into tiny chips.

Wood is made into pulp.

Dyes added to pulp.

Pulp is passed through heated rollers and dried.

Different kinds of modern paper are used for decoration.

Finished paper wound into roll

JAPANESE PAPER
Japanese paper was once made by hand. It was very fine and delicate, and was stored in the form of scrolls. This scroll has been turned into a book by folding it like a concertina.

Veneers

Woods with an attractive grain pattern are sliced into thin layers called veneers. Furniture makers use veneers to cover cheaper woods. Veneers of hard woods are cut with a circular saw. A long sheet of veneer can be cut by rotating a log against a large, stationary blade.

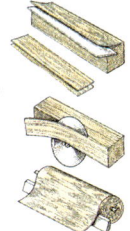

Sawmill

Felling trees and sawing the logs into planks of timber was tremendously hard work. With the introduction of sawmills (such as the one above) most of this work is now done by machines.

Quarter sawing

This is the traditional way to saw a log of high-quality timber. It produces boards that keep their shape without bending or warping, but it is a complicated method and rather wasteful.

Segments are used to make smaller boards.

Paper facts

- It takes more than 2 tonnes (tons) of wood to make just 1 tonne (ton) of paper.
- A person in Western society uses about 120 kg (265 lb) of paper each year.
- Paper was invented in A.D. 105 by a Chinese court official, Tsai Lun.

NORTHERN CONIFEROUS FORESTS

PACIFIC FORESTS

THE STATELY CONIFERS of the forests bordering the Pacific Ocean are among North America's tallest and finest trees. These coastal forests are constantly damp and misty. A thick carpet of ferns and mosses covers the ground and tree trunks.

The pale brown cones are about 8 cm (3 in) long.

SITKA SPRUCE
This sharp-needled spruce grows along moist, coastal lowlands. Although native to North America, it is familiar as a plantation tree elsewhere. The pale soft wood is particularly suitable for paper manufacture.

WESTERN HEMLOCK
This tall tree grows in forests spreading from the coast to the tree line on the western slopes of the Rocky Mountains. Its strap-shaped needles are uneven in length, and the tips of its shoots droop downwards.

PACIFIC FORESTS

LOGGING
In North America and Scandinavia, rivers were traditionally used as a way of transporting felled logs to the sawmill. The heavy trunks were floated down the river and often got stuck. These log jams caused tremendous damage to the riverbanks. Today, logs are usually removed by lorries.

Carved bird protects the tribe

WESTERN RED CEDAR
The leaves of this tree are arranged in flat sprays of tiny, shiny scale leaves that smell fruity when they are bruised.

TOTEM POLE
Native Americans used totem poles to signify the unity of the tribal group. Western red cedar trees were carved into totem poles by the tribes of the north-west.

Totems featured tribal ancestors

Flat sprays of shiny scale leaves

Small clusters of cones contain little winged seeds

57

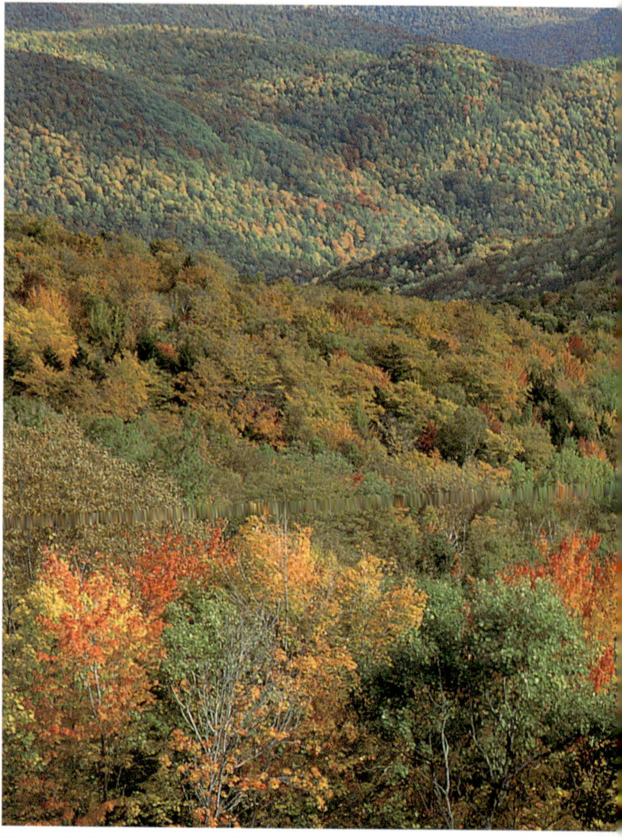

Temperate Forests

The habitat 60
North america 62
The southern states 64
Europe 66
By the river 68
Wetlands 70
Hedges 72
Central europe 74
The balkans 76
The middle east 78
Fruits and nuts 80
Northern china 82
Central china 84
Southern china 86
Japan 88

TEMPERATE FORESTS

THE HABITAT

TEMPERATE FORESTS are found in North America, Europe, and eastern Asia. They consist mostly of deciduous, broadleaved trees that shed their leaves in autumn and spend the winter without them. Summers in these areas are mild, but winters can bring frost and snow.

TAWNY OWL
Old, hollow trees are an important part of the woodland environment. To the tawny owl, for example, they offer an ideal nesting place.

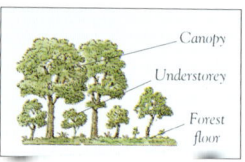

TEMPERATE LAYERS
A temperate forest has three layers. At the top is a canopy of leafy branches. Below this, the understorey consists of woody shrubs and bushes, and young trees, called saplings. The forest floor is covered with grasses, flowers, ferns, and mosses.

ENGLISH ELM
Many trees suffer from attack by insects or types of fungi. For example, Dutch elm disease, a fungal infection, has killed most of the English elms since the 1970s.

WHITE ADMIRAL BUTTERFLY
Deciduous woodlands offer
damp, shady patches that are
ideal for butterflies such as
the white admiral. Adult
butterflies live mostly
in the canopy.
Caterpillars
live on
honeysuckle
around tree
trunks.

Chemical changes make leaves change from green to yellow to red to orange.

CHANGING LEAVES
Leaves produce
brilliant displays
of colour as they
die and fall. On
the forest floor, mites,
bacteria, fungi, and
earthworms break
down the blanket of
fallen leaves into a
dark, crumbly layer
called humus. Humus
improves the texture
and the amount of
food, called nutrients,
in the soil.

HABITAT FACTS

- Temperate woodlands are made up of smaller habitats, such as fallen logs, hollow branches, clearings, mossy stumps, and swampy patches.

- Temperate forests contain over 500 species of oak tree.

- About 15 per cent of the Earth's surface is covered with temperate forests.

LEAF LITTER

61

TEMPERATE FORESTS

NORTH AMERICA

THE DECIDUOUS WOODLANDS of North America are richer than those of Europ During the Ice Age, forests in both continents were pushed south, but North America had no cold mounta ranges to stop them moving north when the ice retreated.

SHAGBARK HICKORY
This hickory gets its name from the shaggy appearance of its bark, which peels off in strips. There are many different species of hickory in North America.

Lobed leaves

BEAVER
Beavers gnaw through tree trunks and use the wood to build dams across streams. Beavers can gnaw through a sapling that is 7½ cm (3 in) across in just 12 minutes. One animal can fell up to 300 trees in a single year.

WHITE OAK
Deeply lobed leaves are a distinctiv feature of the white oak, which is widespread in North American forests. The white oak has good quality timber, which is used for furniture and flooring.

NORTH AMERICA

Collecting syrup
Native Americans taught the first settlers how to prepare sugar and syrup from the sap of the sugar maple. Sap collected from slits in the bark was boiled until it thickened.

The Iroquois Indians used the soft wood of this tree to make "false face" masks.

BASSWOOD

RED MAPLE
In late spring, long-stemmed clusters of winged fruit fall from the red maple. Natural dyes can be obtained from the tree's bark by treating it with iron or aluminium salts. This tree occurs naturally in boggy places.

Each leaf has three or five toothed lobes

Glossy green leaves turn red in autumn

TEMPERATE FORESTS

THE SOUTHERN STATES

THE SOUTH-EASTERN CORNER of the United States contains many freshwater swamps and coastal plains. The climate becomes increasingly warm, with some areas enjoying sub-tropical temperatures. Of the many different tree species that flourish here, some, like the bull bay, are found only in this area.

SPANISH MOSS
Spanish moss is neither Spanish nor a moss. It is a flowering plant that grows on trees in tropical and sub-tropical parts of America.

Very fragrant large, creamy white flowers

Underside of leaf often covered in rust-coloured hairs

Glossy green upperside of leaf

BULL BAY
This tree grows in rich, moist soil beside rivers and lakes. It is a favourite garden tree because of its large, glossy, dark green leaves and creamy white, fragrant flowers, which measure about 30 cm (12 in) across.

BLACK LOCUST
This tall tree has deeply furrowed bark, and pairs of spines scattered along its twigs. The compound leaves are divided into 11 to 21 oval leaflets. Native Americans used the hard, strong wood for bows, and made a blue dye from the leaves.

Each compound leaf is up to 45 cm (18 in) long.

Each leaflet is thinly covered with hairs.

The scented white flowers are arranged in a hanging spike.

GUN MADE FROM BLACK WALNUT

The sweet gum produces winged seeds which are eaten by birds.

BLACK WALNUT
The walnut is a fine but now scarce tree of central and southern United States. Its excellent timber is in great demand for gun stocks and good quality furniture.

SWEET GUM
This tree gets its name from the balsam-scented resin that oozes from cuts in its bark. It grows in damp soils in the southern states.

TEMPERATE FORESTS

EUROPE

DENSE FOREST once covered most of Europe, from the shores of the Mediterranean Sea to Scandinavia. Much of this natural tree cover has been cleared to make way for farming and building. The woodlands that remain provide an essential home for many different kinds of wildlife.

Purple leaves have red leaf stalks

SILVER BIRCH
This ornamental variety is often grown in gardens, and seldom found in the wild. It has purple leaves with red leaf stalks. Its bark has a purplish tinge.

BLUEBELLS
In spring, before the leaves come out, the forest floor is bathed in sunlight. Bluebells and other woodland flowers use this light to grow. Food made by the leaves is stored in bulbs underground.

WOODLAND
Broadleaved beechwoods such as this one produce huge amounts of wood, flowers, fruits, and seeds every year. These provide food for many woodland animals. The trees also help maintain the balance of oxygen and carbon dioxide in the air.

Ancient Greek and Roman kings and emperors wore wreaths of oak leaves.

Many birds' nests are hidden by leafy branches in summer, and can only be seen in winter.

Oak timber was used for ship-building until the beginning of this century.

OAK

The common or English oak is still one of the most important European woodland trees, and often one of the longest-living. Oaks were worshipped by early European peoples such as the Druids. They were also regarded as sacred to the gods of thunder by the Slavic and Teutonic peoples.

ENGLISH OAK

YOUNG ACORNS

TEMPERATE FORESTS

BY THE RIVER

RIVERSIDE TREES get more light than those in a forest, but the soil is often full of water and may lack nutrients. The fruits or seeds of many riverside trees are light enough to float on water as well as on the wind. Riverside tree roots play an important part in preventing the banks from being eroded.

GREY HERON
This large bird stands motionless by the river's edge. It catches fish with a sudden lunge of its long bill.

RIVER BIRCH
Young river birch trees have papery, orange-pink bark, which matures to reddish brown. The river birch is the only lowland birch of the southern United States.

Trumpet-shaped flowers

Large, broad leaves

INDIAN BEAN TREE
Attractive pyramids of purple-spotted white flowers mean that this tree is often grown ornamentally, far away from the riversides of its native south-eastern United States.

Broad leaf tip may be notched

COMMON ALDER
This European tree is common on waterlogged ground beside rivers. It is firmly anchored to the ground by a well-branched root system. Alder flowers are arranged in catkins. Female catkins mature into small, woody cones that open in autumn. They release tiny fruits that float.

Green fruits turn brown when ripe

RIVERBANK WILLOWS
Willows are very graceful riverside trees, with narrow, finely toothed leaves on long, slender twigs. Willow bark contains salicin, an aspirin-like substance that was used for pain relief long before the drug was made artificially.

Willows are often planted on river banks to stop them eroding.

TEMPERATE FORESTS

ALLIGATOR

WETLANDS

THE LOW-LYING COASTAL plains of the south-eastern United States consist of large areas of freshwater swamps. Only a few species of tree can thrive in the waterlogged ground. The swamps are home to the alligator, a large predatory reptile that often lies motionless in the water.

WHITE CYPRESS
This conifer is found growing in swamps near the coast. Its wood is often used to make organ pipes as it produces a very good sound.

Small brown cone with six pointed scales

Leaves turn orange and red in autumn

Tiny, pointed leaves

SWAMP TUPELO
Two kinds of tupelo are found in swamps. Water tupelo grows with the base of its trunk under water. Swamp tupelo, which is also called black gum in the United States, grows beside swamps and in moist woods.

Leaf snaps shut when an insect lands

VENUS FLY TRAP
Nitrates are an essential plant food, but are in short supply in the swampy, acid soil. The Venus fly trap makes up for this by trapping insects that land on its leaves. The insect is turned into a "soup" that is absorbed through the leaf surface.

Trunk becomes narrower as it rises

SWAMP CYPRESS
The swamp cypress is a deciduous conifer. Its tall, thin trunk is wider, or buttressed, at the bottom to provide anchorage in the wet mud.

HEDGES

A HEDGE IS a narrow strip of vegetation made up of woody shrubs. Trees called standards grow along the length of the hedge. Thorny scramblers, such as brambles, together with species such as wild roses and bryony, bind the hedge into a thick barrier. Several colourful wild flowers grow along the hedge bank.

ROSEHIPS AND THEIR SEEDS ATTRACT BIRDS IN WINTER

MARKING BOUNDARIES
People plant hedges to mark the boundaries between fields and farms, and to enclose farm animals. Hedges that are properly maintained can last for hundreds of years, although it is often difficult to date old hedges accurately.

Pruning along the top only (above) means no new twigs grow at the base.

HEDGE LAYING
Hedgerow trees and bushes are traditionally pruned and pinned down to encourage dense, twiggy growth (far left). Today, most farmers use mechanical flails to trim the tops and sides of hedges.

HEDGES

HEDGE FACTS

- The word "hedge" comes from the Anglo-Saxon "heog" meaning a territorial boundary.
- Small fields bordered by hedges are a traditional feature of the British countryside.
- Hedges are valuable to wildlife when they link blocks of woodland.

HEDGES AND WILDLIFE

A hedge provides a good habitat for a rich variety of wildlife. Small birds feed and nest in its twiggy branches. Voles, mice, and weasels are among the mammals that live in the well-drained hedgebank. The hedgerow attracts numerous insects in summer, and in winter, its seeds and berries are a valuable source of food for many birds and animals.

Thick shrubs are ideal for nesting birds.

Hawthorn is an important hedgerow species because it tolerates a wide range of soils.

HAWTHORN

HOLLY

TEMPERATE FORESTS

CENTRAL EUROPE

THE POLISH FOREST of Bialowieza is all that remains of the natural woodland that once covered most of central Europe. Much of this area still has plenty of mixed woodlands, with both coniferous and deciduous trees. However, farming and a rising human population have greatly reduced their numbers.

Effects of acid rain in Germany's Black Forest

ACID RAIN
Trees, lakes, rivers, and plants are all affected by acid rain. It is formed when industrial chemicals such as sulphur dioxide and nitrogen oxides mix with moisture in the air.

SILVER FIR
This tree is very common in Germany. The pale bands beneath each dark, glossy, strap-shaped leaf show as a flash of silver when the wind blows through its branches.

CENTRAL EUROPE

COMMON BEECH
The beech is an important forest tree. Its timber is ideal for furniture and kitchen utensils. The beech was one of the Celt's sacred trees.

Wavy, untoothed leaf margin

THE RHINE
Marksburg Castle is near the river Rhine in Germany. Like many other medieval castles, it was built on top of a rocky, heavily wooded slope, which offered protection against attack.

The oldest part of the castle is its central tower

BLACK POPLAR
A mature black poplar is a massive tree that is often found beside rivers. It has large lumps of rough bark on its trunk, and heavy branches that curve downwards. Male and female catkins grow on separate trees.

TEMPERATE FORESTS

THE BALKANS

THE SOUTH-EASTERN CORNER of Europe enjoys long, hot summers, which are ideal for growing fruits such as cherries and plums. To prevent the loss of water, the leaves of some trees droop or fold during the hottest part of the day. Winters in this area are very cold, with thick snowfalls, especially over the mountains.

ORIENTAL PLANE TREE

Yellow flower blotch becomes red

Unstalked leaflets

CONKERS
The fruits of the horse chestnut tree have a thick spiny coat, and look a little like medieval clubs. Inside are one to three shiny brown seeds that children often use to play a game called conkers.

HORSE CHESTNUT
Spikes of creamy coloured flowers, which are often called "candles", appear on this tree in early summer. Each leaf is palmate, and is made up of large, toothed leaflets. The leaves form a dense, spreading crown.

76

THE BALKANS

Deeply lobed leaf

Tree has pale grey bark

(HU)NGARIAN OAK
(Th)is oak is widespread from Italy across the (Bal)kans and Hungary. It has very distinctive (lea)ves, with up to 20 lobes each, and grows (ver)y quickly in good conditions.

(You)ng leaves (c)ompletely (co)vered with (w)hite hairs

Dark green upper surface of leaf

Strong shoots bear maple-like leaves

White, (c)ottony (low)er surface

WHITE POPLAR
Even in places that are usually very hot and dry, white poplars (will) grow along the riverside. The young leaves (are) white with cottony hairs that stop them from (dry)ing in the sun. Mature leaves are dark green (on t)op, but keep a coating of hairs underneath.

WHITE POPLAR TREE

TEMPERATE FORESTS

THE MIDDLE EAST

MUCH OF THE MIDDLE EAST is desert or arid, but in the north, the climate is wetter, especially over the mountains and near the Black and Caspian Seas. Forests once flourished here, as well as in the Lebanon and the once fertile river valleys of Iraq. Many of these forests have been destroyed by farming. True forest can now be found only on inaccessible slopes.

CAUCASIAN WINGNUT
This tree grows in wet soils beside rivers. It has a short trunk, and a spreading crown with large, pinnate leaves.

Leaves fold inwards towards midrib

ROMAN IVORY BOX

JUDAS TREE
This Roman ivory box was carved in A.D. 420. It shows the crucifix of Christ, with Judas Iscariot, his betrayer, hanging from a nearby tree. This tree later became known as the Judas tree. The Judas tree small tree with heart-shaped leav and bright pink, pea-like flowers.

THE MIDDLE EAST

TURKISH HAZEL
This hazel grows in shady forested valleys. Male flowers are in catkins, while the tiny female flowers are almost completely hidden in buds. The fruit is encased in a leafy husk. It has a hard shell and contains a single large seed – a hazelnut.

Long, drooping male catkins

Smooth, oval leaves are heart-shaped at the bottom

CEDAR OF LEBANON
This distinctive tree was once part of forests growing on the slopes of Lebanese mountains. Its timber made it one of the most important trees of the Middle East.

Broad, flattened sprays of branches

EGYPTIAN BOAT
The Egyptians were importing cedar from Lebanon by 3000 B.C. The wood was used to make boats, and the resin from the trunks was used to preserve dead bodies. This process is called embalming.

TEMPERATE FORESTS

FRUITS AND NUTS

THE SWEET, JUICY fruits that we know today are descended from wild fruit trees. Wild fruits are often small and sour. However, over the centuries, wild fruit trees have been selected and improved to produce much larger and sweeter varieties.

CITRUS FRUITS
Oranges and lemons both originated in southern China. Today they are grown in many countries that have a warm, frost-free climate. Orange trees are small, with glossy leaves. They produce fragrant white flowers as well as juicy fruits.

ORANGE TREE

PISTACHIO NUTS
Pistachios are the seeds of a small, deciduous tree that is native to the Middle East, but is also grown in other parts of the world. The nuts are famous as ingredients in Middle Eastern sweets such as Turkish delight.

These nuts are also roasted and eaten as a snack.

FRUITS AND NUTS

Single, hard stone typical of stone fruit

STONE FRUITS
Plums and peaches are stone fruits, so called because their juicy flesh covers a large "stone". Peaches came originally from China, but plums probably came from western Asia.

FRUIT FACTS

- Ancient Egyptians were the first people to cultivate cherries, about 2,700 years ago.

- There are over 6,000 different kinds of apple. Over 23 million tonnes (tons) of apples are produced each year.

- Over 30 million tonnes (tons) of oranges are grown every year. Many of these are made into orange juice.

PEARS
These succulent fruits have descended from wild pear trees that grow in western Asia and Europe. Like apples, pears contain a core that has several small pips.

ORCHARDS
Traditional orchards were full of tall fruit trees in widely spaced rows. The fruit was hand-picked. In modern orchards, special dwarf varieties are planted close together. The fruit is closer to the ground and easier to pick.

TEMPERATE FORESTS

NORTHERN CHINA

MUCH OF NORTHERN CHINA is flat and dry, with a covering of grasses and desert plants that can survive periods of drought. To the east and west of this area however there are also mountain ranges. Here, forests of pines, spruces, and firs cover the slopes. Hardy broadleaved trees flourish in the more sheltered valleys.

KOREAN PINE
This hardy pine grows on the lower mountain slopes and along river valleys.

Thick, corky amur tree bark has medicinal uses in China.

AMUR CORK TREE FRUITS

Leaves have a glossy green upperside.

AMUR CORK TREE
This is a broad, spreading tree that grows along mountain-side streams. It has pinnate leaves with glossy leaflets. Both the leaves and fruit have a pleasant smell. When ripe, the fruits turn from green to black.

NORTHERN CHINA

Cone scales have wavy margins.

Green unripe cone

ACUPUNCTURE
The Chinese have used the practice of acupuncture to cure illness and provide pain relief for over 2,000 years. These acupuncture needles are stored in a mahogany case, and date back to the 19th century.

YEZO SPRUCE
The Yezo spruce grows in the subalpine slopes and dry upland plateaux of north-east Asia and Japan. It is tall with a narrow crown and short, flat needles that point forwards. Its reddish-brown, drooping cones are 7½ cm (3 in) long.

SOUTHERN MINSHAN MOUNTAINS
Dense forests of conifers cover the slopes of these mountains in northern China. The crowns of the firs and spruces here are tall and very narrow because the trees grow so close together. In the sheltered valleys seen in the foreground, small broadleaved trees and bushes flourish.

TEMPERATE FORESTS

CENTRAL CHINA

DURING THE LAST ICE AGE, whole forests were killed by the cold, and many tree species became extinct. In isolated parts of China, however, a few species survived. These include trees that are now the only living representatives of groups that were once widespread.

CHINESE SPIRITS
Chinese civilizations are rich in folklore. The Chinese believe that each tree has a spirit, which often attacks woodcutters.

Winged fruits are green

CHINESE WING-NUT
This tree grows in moist woodlands. Its tiny flowers have no petals, and are borne in catkins. When the winged fruits develop, these catkins grow to 30 cm (12 in).

Short, pointed leaflets

Leaves turn yellow in autumn

DAWN REDWOOD
This conifer was known only as a 100 million-year-old fossil until a Chinese forester found three living trees in 1941. More trees were found in 1944.

8 4

CENTRAL CHINA

Sharply toothed leaves

Leaves are like two-lobed fans with veins that spread out from the base.

Rounded base

KEAKI
The keaki is an important timber tree in both China and Japan. Its wood is used to build furniture and boats. The keaki is a riverside tree, and grows best in deep, rich soils.

MAIDENHAIR TREE
This is the only remaining member of a family of trees that was widespread 150–200 million years ago. Truly wild maidenhair trees are found in the Tianmu mountains, but for centuries the Chinese have planted these trees around their temples. The maidenhair is grouped with conifers, although it is considered more primitive.

TEMPERATE FORESTS

SOUTHERN CHINA

THE SOUTHERN REGIONS of China are almost sub-tropical, although it is cooler on the higher mountain slopes of the south-west. A rich variety of tree species flourish, many of which have attractive blossoms or edible fruits. However, large areas of the lowlands have been cleared because of the need to grow crops such as rice, soybeans, and lichees.

PYRUS CALLERYANA
This wild pear tree has tiny, white-spotted brown fruits.

Few trees can grow on the steep, craggy slopes

SOUTHERN CHINA

MAGNOLIA DELAVAYI
This magnolia grows in open sites or at the edge of forests. It is a broadly spreading, small tree with fragrant, creamy coloured flowers that open in the evening to attract the night-flying moths that pollinate it.

Rich, glossy dark green leaves

CHINESE BOX
This 17th-century lacquered box depicts a weeping willow. These graceful trees often feature in Chinese art, as the willow is seen as a symbol of meekness by Buddhists.

TYPICAL SCENE
In the province of Yangshuo, southern China, conifers and broadleaved trees grow near the banks of rivers in mountainous regions.

JAPAN

JAPAN IS A COUNTRY of islands and mountains, and the trees that grow there reflect the contrasts in its landscape and climate. For example, Hokkaido in the north is very cold, but to the south, the climate is sub-tropical.

JAPANESE MAPLE

Japanese broadleaves

Hardy birches, willows, and alders grow in the colder parts of northern Japan. Central Japan is warmer, and here deciduous broadleaved trees flourish. Evergreen broadleaved trees, including many kinds of laurel, are found on the sub-tropical southern islands.

KATSURA TREE
This is the tallest Japanese broadleaved tree. It has furrowed, flaking bark and a spreading crown of round, toothed leaves. These turn a clear lemon yellow in autumn.

JAPAN

SIKA DEER
These deer live in the mixed woodlands of eastern Asia and Japan, where there is plenty of undergrowth. They emerge at dawn and dusk to feed. The spotted young hide among trees or tall plants until they are strong enough to escape from danger.

SOUNKYO GORGE, HOKKAIDO
This steep-sided gorge in the north of Japan has natural "bonsai" trees clinging to narrow crevices. Japanese gardeners recreate these wild scenes in parks and temple grounds.

Young leaves are a deep bronze colour

Flowers from this variety do not turn into fruit.

PRUNUS SERRULATA "KANZAN"
Japan is famous for its flowering cherries, which have been cultivated there for centuries. Many of these ornamental varieties have double flowers of frilly petals.

TEMPERATE FORESTS

Japanese conifers

The rugged landscape of much of Japan is clothed with hardy conifer trees. In autumn, their dark foliage mingles with splashes of colour from nearby broadleaved trees. One of the most important trees in Japan is the Japanese cedar. It grows in natural forests and in plantations. It is prized for its timber, and can live for over a thousand years.

SHINZU MAEDA FOREST
The Japanese cedars of Shinzu Maeda forest have tall, unbranched trunks topped with a narrow crown high above the ground.

JAPANESE CEDAR
The trunk of this tall tree is covered with stringy bark. It has very short, slender needles that point forwards. The tiny cones look like spiky balls.

GOLDEN TEMPLE, KYOTO
Temple gardens are carefully landscaped to encourage meditation and serenity. The trees growing here are pines.

JAPAN

VEITCH'S FIR
This is the smallest Japanese fir. Its upturned needles reveal bright silvery bands on their lower surface. It has resinous, purplish buds, and the upright cones are also purple when ripe.

TYPICAL FOREST SCENE
This view of Daisetsuzan National Park shows one of the highest peaks of Hokkaido. Forests of conifers – spruces, firs, and pines – together with hardy broadleaved trees, cover its lower slopes.

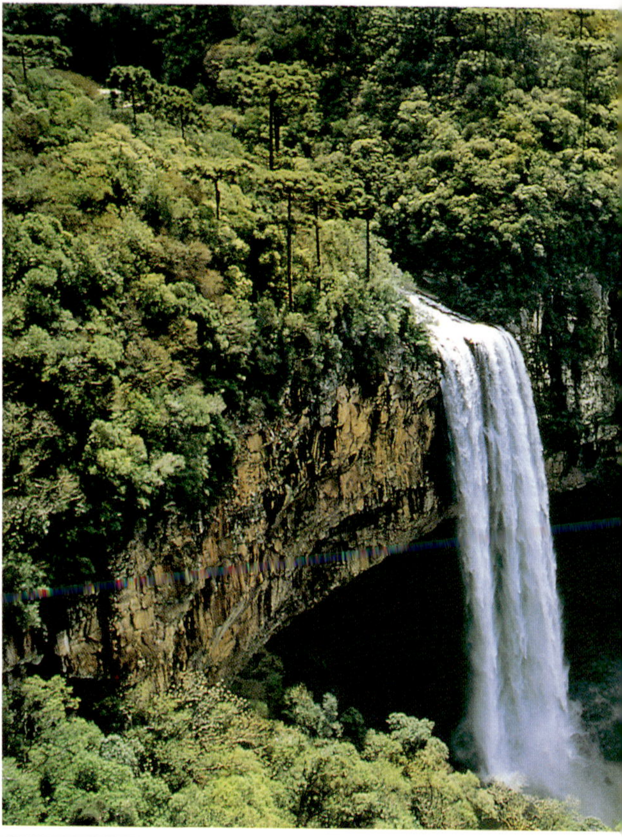

Tropical Forests

The habitat 94
America 96
Tropical products 98
Tropical africa 100
Tropical asia 102
Mist forests 104
Australia 106

TROPICAL FORESTS

THE HABITAT

THE TROPICAL REGION is a zone around the Equator. It stretches from the Tropic of Cancer in the north to the Tropic of Capricorn in the south. Here, the year is divided into wet and dry seasons. The climate is warm and often humid. In the wetter parts of the tropics, dense rainforests cover huge areas of land.

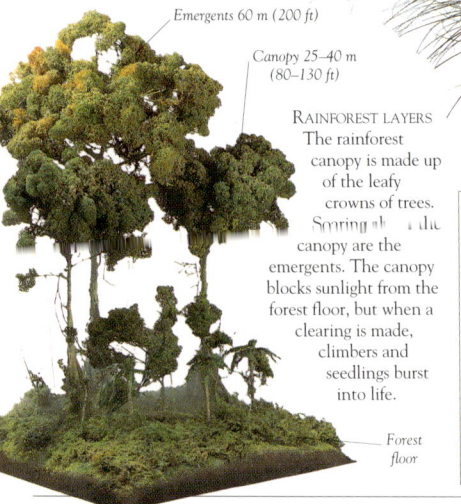

Emergents 60 m (200 ft)

Canopy 25–40 m (80–130 ft)

RAINFOREST LAYERS
The rainforest canopy is made up of the leafy crowns of trees. Soaring above the canopy are the emergents. The canopy blocks sunlight from the forest floor, but when a clearing is made, climbers and seedlings burst into life.

Forest floor

TROPICAL FACTS
- Tropical rainforest grows where there is little or no dry season, and at least 2000 mm (80 in) of rain a year.
- Seasonal (monsoon) forests are found in areas with a dry season of 3 months or more.
- Tropical savannahs have a brief rainy season once a year.

THE HABITAT

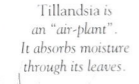

Tillandsia is an "air-plant". It absorbs moisture through its leaves.

Anthurium salviniae belongs to a family of plants called aroids. Water runs down the leaf stalks to the fibrous root mat.

Liana
Climbing plants that grow up rainforest trees are called lianas. Some climb up trunks, others have stems that twine around each other.

Epiphytes
Plants that sit on the branches of tropical rainforest trees are called epiphytes. Although rainforests get a lot of rain, the water drains away quickly. Epiphytes therefore have thick, waxy leaves to reduce water loss. The leaves are often arranged like a funnel to channel water down to their roots. Some species of epiphyte also have leaves that absorb moisture directly from the air.

These orchid leaves are thick and glossy to prevent water loss through evaporation.

TROPICAL FORESTS

AMERICA

CENTRAL AND SOUTH America are home to the largest, richest tropical rainforests in the world. There are more species of tree in the vast Amazon basin than anywhere else in the world. Lowland rainforest covers most of this area, with mangroves fringing the coastline.

Bright, conspicuous flowers bring splashes of colour to the green canopy of the rainforest.

KAPOK TREE
The kapok is a native American tree. Its seeds are embedded in fluffy fibres that burst out when the fruit splits. They are dispersed by winds that blow high above the canopy.

CANOPY
Broadleaved trees and palms make up the canopy of the rainforests in this area. It always appear green and leafy, but many of the trees are leafless for brief periods of the year

CUVIER'S TOUCAN
This toucan lives high up in rainforest trees and nests in tree holes. It uses its large, light beak to pick ripe fruits. Small berries are swallowed whole, but larger fruits are pecked apart.

MONTANE FOREST
On the slopes of the Andes Mountains in South America, lowland forest changes to montane forest. It is cooler here, but still very wet. The trees do not grow as tall, and are covered with mosses, ferns, liverworts, and beautiful orchids.

Carapa has a compound leaf, divided into several glossy leaflets

CARAPA GUIANENSIS
This tree is found in Central and South America. It grows in swampy ground, or in parts of a forest that are often flooded. It has large corky fruits that float. The seeds also float, and those that are not eaten by animals germinate quickly into tall seedlings.

TROPICAL PRODUCTS

TREES OF THE TROPICS provide the world with an array of products, from chocolate to rubber. Although some products are still harvested from natural forests, others come from trees grown in plantations.

OIL PALM
Oil pressed from the fruit pulp of this African tree is used to make margarine and candles.

PAWPAW
Pawpaw, or papaya, is a sweet, juicy fruit from Central America. It is one of the fruit trees most often planted in the tropics.

CINNAMON
Cinnamon spice comes from the bark of young cinnamon trees. When it is left to dry, the bark curls up. The cinnamon tree is native to India and Sri Lanka.

CINNAMON STICKS

BRAZIL NUTS
Wild trees in the Amazonian forest produce brazil nuts. The woody fruits fall from the tree when ripe, and are gathered from the ground. Inside each fruit are between 15 and 30 hard-shelled nuts that are rich in oils and protein.

Hard shell protects nut inside

TROPICAL PRODUCTS

CHOCOLATE
Cocoa beans are roasted, shelled, and ground into cocoa mass. This is a rich fatty substance from which chocolate, cocoa, and cocoa butter are made.

COCOA PODS
Cocoa beans are the seeds of a small tree from the tropical American jungles. When ripe, the fruit pods are picked and the seeds are removed. The seeds are then washed and dried, ready to be made into cocoa products.

Seeds embedded in pulp

Thick rind of fruit pod

Empty husk

COFFEE TREE
This tree is native to Africa. Each coffee "cherry" contains two seeds. These are roasted to produce the familiar coffee beans.

COFFEE TREE

COFFEE BEANS

TROPICAL FACTS

- More than 1,200 thousand tonnes (tons) of cocoa beans are produced every year.

- More than 4,800 thousand tonnes (tons) of coffee beans are produced each year.

- More than 4,500 thousand tonnes (tons) of dried coconut flesh are produced each year.

TROPICAL FORESTS

Tropical Africa

TROPICAL AFRICA is a mixture of rainforest, desert and savannah. Many different species of broadleaved and palm trees grow in the rainforests. Trees in scrub and desert areas are often stunted and sparse. Savannah trees have extremely deep roots to tap water far underground. This allows them to survive the long dry season.

WATTLED BLACK HORNBILL
This large hornbill lives in rainforests, where it can find fruit all year round.

TROPICAL AFRICA

WHISTLING THORN
Only the most drought-resistant trees, such as the whistling thorn acacia, can survive on the African savannah grasslands. Its long roots tap stores of underground water.

CANDELABRA TREE
The thick, green branches of the candelabra tree act as leaves. This helps the tree to conserve water. It gets its name from the curious shape of the crown, which is formed as the outer branches continue to grow upwards.

Insects and animals flock to feed on the white flowers and woody-shelled, pulpy fruits.

Hollows in the massive trunk provide nesting sites for birds such as barn owls.

BAOBAB
The amazing baobab can store about 9,000 litres (2,400 gallons) of water in its swollen trunk. This enables it to survive in the hot dry climate of the savannah. Some baobabs live for over 3,000 years. They attract numerous species of birds, insects, and fruit bats.

TROPICAL ASIA

THE TROPICAL JUNGLES of mainland Asia, the Philippines, and Sri Lanka once consisted of huge areas of dipterocarp and teak trees. Much of this area has now been felled for timber and agriculture. In contrast, much of the lowland and montane rainforests of Borneo and New Guinea are inaccessible, and have remained largely unspoilt.

PEEPUL TREE
Revered and planted beside Buddhist temples, the peepul tree is the tree of great wisdom, under which Buddha received enlightenment. It is a broadly spreading tree, and in Sri Lanka, a whole village of a hundred huts once dwelt beneath a single peepul tree.

Tualang stretches above the rest of the jungle

TUALANG
The tualang can reach heights of up to 75 m (245 ft), and is the tallest tree in the tropical Malaysian jungle. Local people do not like to fell the tualang, as they believe that spirits live in its crown. Wild bees build their honeycombs hanging from the tualang's branches, well out of reach of the honey-loving sun bears that roam this area.

TROPICAL ASIA

BANYAN TREE
This curious fig tree sends numerous roots down to the ground from its spreading branches. There can be hundreds of such roots, which thicken and look like extra trunks. In this way, the banyan can spread to cover huge areas – a crown 600 m (2,000 ft) in circumference was recorded from a banyan near Poona, India.

Long, muscular arms for swinging through trees in the jungle

ALOCASIA THIBAUTANIA

Each long-stalked leaf has silvery veins on its upper side, and is purple underneath.

ORANG-UTAN
In Malay, orang-utan means "man of the forest" – which is an apt description of this large ape. Orang-utans live only in Borneo and Sumatra. Each one needs a large area of undisturbed jungle in which to forage for fruit. Adults seek each other's company only to mate.

AROID
This forest floor plant is a kind of arum lily. On the underside of its leaves is a purple pigment. This helps it to make the best use of the limited light on the floor of the South-east Asian jungle.

TROPICAL FORESTS

Mist forests

THE EVERGREEN RAINFORESTS of tropical mountainsides are not the same as the jungles of surrounding lowlands. These are the montane forests, also known as mist or cloud forests because they are always shrouded in low cloud. The trees in these damp, cool forests are different from those in lowland rainforests.

TREE KANGAROO

RAINFOREST LEVELS
The temperature falls by about 0.6°C (1.1°F) every 100 m (330 ft) climbed up a mountainside. At about 1,000 m (3,300 ft), cool montane forests replace warm rainforests.

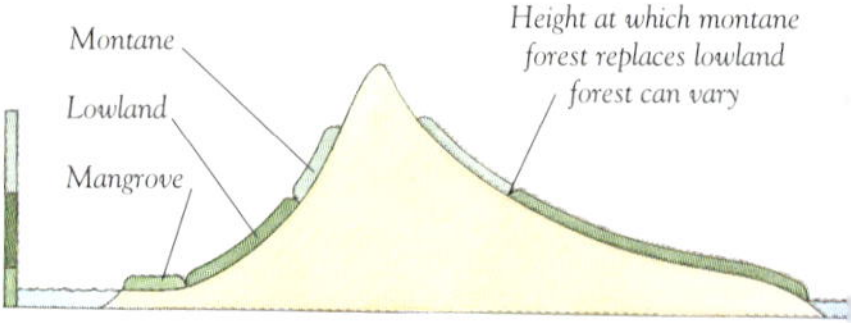

Montane
Lowland
Mangrove

Height at which montane forest replaces lowland forest can vary

CAMERON HIGHLANDS
The steeper sides of the Cameron Highlands in Malaysia are thickly covered in cloud forests. Moisture condenses out of the cool, damp air, and drops from the foilage. Although flatter areas of the highlands have been cleared for farming, natural forests still flourish on steep or inaccessible slopes.

The male lifts up his tail as part of a courtship display.

KING BIRD OF PARADISE
Male king birds of paradise gather among the mist forest trees in groups called leks. Their shimmering displays attract the more dowdy female birds.

Trunks and branches are festooned with mosses and liverworts.

INSIDE A MIST FOREST
In the cool, moist air of a mist forest, thin-leaved plants such as mosses and liverworts cover almost every surface.

TROPICAL FORESTS

AUSTRALIA

DESERT AND ARID SAVANNAH grassland make up most of tropical Australia, with narrow patches of rainforest along the east coast. Acacia and eucalyptus trees grow in the hot, tropical grasslands. The rainforest trees include some primitive species of broadleaved trees and conifers.

KOALA

GHOST GUM
Ghost gums are scattered throughout most of tropical Australia, along the banks of dry desert riverbeds. Their bark is covered with a white powdery layer that comes off when touched.

Pointed leaves have a thick cuticle to stop them drying out.

Richly flavoured honey is obtained from the small flowers.

White powder bark

AUSTRALIA

STRANGLER FIG
The seeds of a strangler fig germinate at the base of a branch, high up in the crown of a rainforest tree. The small fig plant quickly sends roots down to the soil, where they spread and grow. The fig eventually kills its host.

A fig kills its host by overshadowing the host's leaves and strangling its trunk.

EUCALYPTS
There are perhaps 600 species of eucalypt in Australia. Those that grow in the hotter, drier regions can survive drought, poor soils, and bushfires. After a fire, buds beneath the bark of some varieties sprout and grow, replacing the burnt branches.

Male and female cones grow on separate trees, on the upper branches only.

Symmetrical, domed crown of lance-shaped leaves

BUNYA PINE
The bunya pine grows in rainforest areas in Queensland. It is not a true pine, but is related to the monkey puzzle tree. In each female cone there are up to 150 seeds, which are edible.

Branches usually grow from the trunk in whorls.

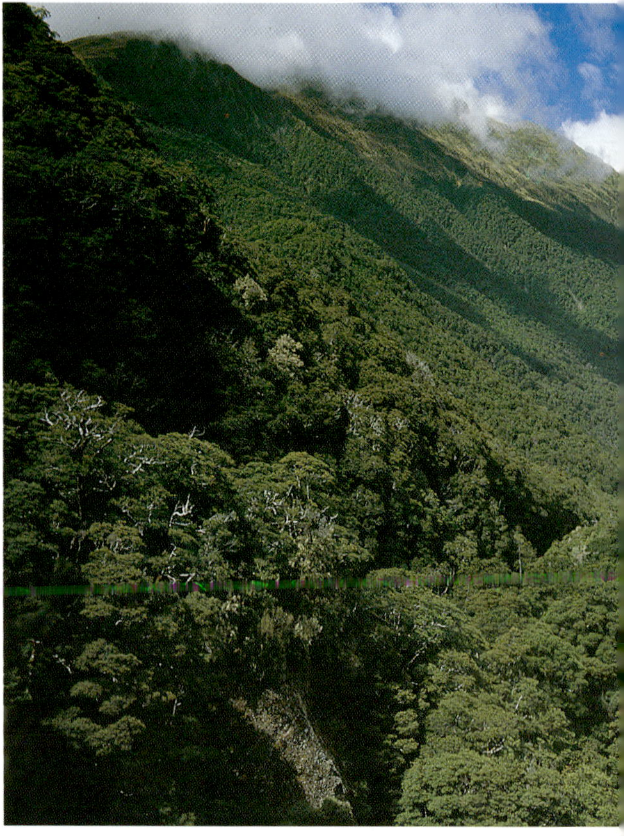

Mixed Evergreen Forests

The habitat 110
South-east Australia 112
New Zealand 114
California 116
South America 118
Mediterranean 120

MIXED EVERGREEN FORESTS

THE HABITAT

THESE FORESTS ARE a mixture of conifers and broadleaved trees. They are found in temperate regions of the world, where the winters are cool but not harsh enough to make the broadleaved trees shed their leaves in winter.

GROUND PARROT

TREE FERNS
In the understorey of moist southern forests, there are tree ferns similar to those growing millions of years ago. Fern spores need damp conditions to grow into new plants.

HOLM OAK
Trees of hot, dry climates, such as this holm oak, have tough, waxy leaves that prevent water loss. Hairs on young leaves and underneath older leaves also help to trap water vapour.

White, hairy young shoots

Male catkins open on young shoots

Tough waxy leaves

HABITAT FACTS
• Pines growing in California and the Mediterranean need scorching sunlight or natural fires to crack open their cones.

• Some of the world's tallest trees grow in these forests. For example, kauris in New Zealand can reach over 75 m (246 ft) tall.

THE HABITAT

KOWHAI
Many similar tree and flower species flourish in the forests of Chile and New Zealand. The kowhai, for example, is found in both countries, growing high up on mountainsides and down to sea level.

Yellow flowers develop into winged seedpods

MOSS
Mosses are a common feature of damp forest floors. They absorb moisture through their leaves as they grow. Their fine rootlets are for attachment only.

SOUTHERN BEECHES
This is a group of 35-40 species of tree, all of which are found in the Southern Hemisphere. They evolved and became widespread at a time when South America, Antarctica, Australia, and New Zealand were all joined together in one landmass called Gondwanaland.

111

MIXED EVERGREEN FORESTS

South-east australia

The south-eastern corner of mainland Australia and the island of Tasmania have rich forests of eucalypts, southern beeches, and some unusual conifers. Southern beeches are the last remnants of the kind of forests that once covered Antarctica.

Summit cedar
This scale-leaved conifer grows on the summits of the Western Mountains, Tasmania.

Kookaburra
The laughing call of the kookaburra, the world's largest kingfisher, is the signature tune of the eastern eucalyptus forests. The kookaburra is a voracious hunter of small snakes, lizards, and insects.

Forest scene
Beneath spreading eucalyptus trees, there is a thick undergrowth of tree ferns and unusual plants such as grass trees.

SOUTH-EAST AUSTRALIA

CIDER GUM
Young eucalyptus leaves are often rounded, stalkless, and grow opposite each other. These are very different from the adult leaves, which are stalked, spear-shaped, and alternate. Cider gum gets its name from the cider-like drink that was made from its sap.

MOUNTAIN ASH
This eucalypt grows in Victoria and Tasmania, and prefers deep, rich soils. It holds the record for the tallest standing broadleaved tree – 95 m (312 ft) high.

Eucalyptus leaves contain oil

Each flower has tiny yellow petals and a mass of stamens.

SILVER WATTLE
This small tree grows in valleys and beside streams. It has feathery leaves with tiny leaflets, and fragrant clusters of "powder-puff" flowers.

Leaves are bipinnate, with tiny leaflets

MIXED EVERGREEN FORESTS

NEW ZEALAND

THE COLLECTION OF TREES found in New Zealand is unlike that found anywhere else. North Island has the warmest climate, and, before the arrival of the Maoris, was covered with huge coniferous forests. In South Island, the climate is cooler, and more moist. Evergreen southern beeches, similar to those found in Chile and Argentina, flourish here.

BOAT BUILDING
The first settlers on New Zealand were the Polynesians. They carved elaborate prowboards for their boats out of local wood.

KAURI
This massive conifer has a tall, wide trunk with a broad, spreading crown. It can live for 2,000 years or more. The kauri is the source of many legends.

Each flower is about 4 cm (1 ½ in) across

Smooth, grey bark

NEW ZEALAND

Single-toothed, smooth leaves

BLACK BEECH
The Maori name for this evergreen broadleaved tree is "Tawhairauriki". Black beech is widespread on mountain slopes and lowlands.

MOUNTAIN RIBBONWOOD
Sprays of creamy white flowers adorn this tree in summer, and the seeds are contained in small, winged capsules. The deciduous leaves are oval or heart-shaped. This tree grows in the understorey of forest clearings.

Yellow buds open into white flowers

A COOL RAINFOREST
A New Zealand rainforest is cool and moist inside, but the temperature is never cold enough for frost. This allows the luxuriant growth of ferns and tree ferns, and almost every surface is covered by mosses and liverworts.

MIXED EVERGREEN FORESTS

CALIFORNIA

MUCH OF CALIFORNIA is dry, or has a low rainfall. To the south are the parched plains of the Mohave Desert, and the sparse scrub and stunted trees of the chaparral. Forests flourish where the climate is more moist, such as along the coast and on mountain slopes.

BIG-CONE PINE

Green, glossy, leathery leaves

MADRONA
These creamy white flowers will turn into rough, reddish berries 1 cm (about ½ in) across. The madrona prefers moist soils in steep canyons or coastal cliffs.

Flowers have sepals instead of petals. These are yellow-green.

CALIFORNIAN LAUREL
In moist, sheltered places, this tree is large and impressive, but in dry, arid sites, it is only a small shrub. Its leaves have a heavy acrid or fruity smell, which is poisonous and can cause headaches. The wood from this tree is used for carving bowls.

116

CALIFORNIA

Cone scales spread out after cone ripens

INCENSE CEDAR
Small scale leaves with sharp tips grow in flattened sprays on this tall conifer. When crushed, the leaves have an aromatic smell. The vase-shaped cones have six woody scales. The wood is also aromatic, and is often made into chests and decorative boxes.

Small scale leaves on flattened spray

MONTEREY CYPRESSES
Monterey cypresses occur naturally only in a small area south of Monterey Bay, California. They are small and stunted in their native habitat, but grow much taller in other parts of the world.

MIXED EVERGREEN FORESTS

SOUTH AMERICA

EVERGREEN FORESTS of southern beeches and conifers flourish on the slopes of the Andes Mountains in Chile and western Argentina. The western slopes face the Pacific Ocean, and are constantly bathed in mist and rain. The eastern slopes of the Andes are much drier.

FOSSILIZED MONKEY PUZZLE CONE

MONKEY PUZZLE TREE
This curious conifer is often seen in parks and gardens, but is in fact native to the eastern slopes of the Andes Mountains. Its distinctive shape makes it easy to recognize.

Sharply pointed, triangular leaves

Tall trunk with wrinkled bark

SOUTH AMERICA

PATAGONIAN CYPRESS
This is one of the few cypresses to grow naturally in the Southern Hemisphere. Its reddish bark peels off in strips. Many of these trees have now been felled for their good-quality timber.

Beak chisels holes in tree trunks

Leaves in whorls of threes

Leaf tips are blunt

ANDEAN FLICKER
This South American woodpecker uses its strong beak to search for food in tree trunks. Its clawed feet are specially adapted for climbing.

Small, rounded brown cone

Stamens have orange anthers

ULMO
The cool, rain-soaked forests of parts of Chile are home to the ulmo. On low ground, it is a tall tree with a narrow crown. Higher up on the mountainsides, it is a much smaller shrub.

Large, white four-petalled flowers are sweetly scented

MIXED EVERGREEN FORESTS

MEDITERRANEAN

NATURAL FORESTS once covered the lands around the Mediterranean Sea. These forests were among the first trees to be cleared by expanding populations of Egyptians, Ancient Greeks, and Romans.

STRAWBERRY TREE
Clusters of small, greenish-white flowers hang among the glossy evergreen leaves of the strawberry tree. The tree's fruits look like tiny strawberries.

Mediterranean broadleaves

In ancient times, wooden ships were vital to the success of nations such as the Greeks and Romans, and many Mediterranean trees were felled as a result. Today, many of the trees here are a valuable food source. Carob tree fruits, for example, are often used as a chocolate substitute.

BAY TREE
To the Ancient Greeks and Romans, the bay was a symbol of wisdom and glory. Its leaves were used for the "crown of laurels" worn by emperors, victors, and important citizens such as magistrates.

MEDITERRANEAN

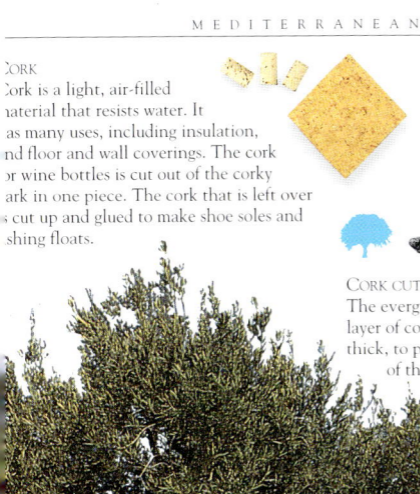

CORK
Cork is a light, air-filled material that resists water. It has many uses, including insulation, and floor and wall coverings. The cork for wine bottles is cut out of the corky bark in one piece. The cork that is left over is cut up and glued to make shoe soles and fishing floats.

CORK CUTTING
The evergreen cork oak produces a layer of corky bark about 7 cm (3 in) thick, to protect the living tissues of the trunk from the Sun's heat. The cork is stripped about every ten years.

OLIVE TREE
The olive tree has been grown around the Mediterranean for at least 5,000 years. The trees can live for up to 1,000 years, and yield large crops of oily fruits. Olive oil is pressed from the fresh fruits.

OLIVE FRUITS

Green olives are picked before they ripen.

MIXED EVERGREEN FORESTS

Mediterranean conifers

Groves of conifers are a familiar sight on the hillsides and mountain slopes of Greece, Italy, and many of the Mediterranean islands. Beneath the shelter of these pines, a rich variety of evergreen shrubs flourish. In areas that are too rocky for trees to grow, there lies a mat of plants that can survive on little water. These often have spiny or strongly scented leaves.

Leaves are borne singly on long shoots

Male cones ripen and shed pollen

EMBLEM OF DEATH
Pluto was the Roman King of the Underworld and God of the Dead. He carried a two-pronged fork as an emblem of his power, and was associated with the dark-leaved cypress tree.

Slender, needle-like leaves

ATLAS CEDAR
This attractive tree grows on the slopes of the Atlas Mountains of Algeria and Morocco. Its sharply pointed needles have a bluish tinge. This makes the Atlas cedar a popular ornamental tree.

MEDITERRANEAN

STONE PINE CONE
The round, heavy cone of the stone pine is up to 10 cm (4 in) long, and has smooth scales. The seeds contain edible kernels, which are known as pine nuts.

PINE KERNELS

PINE CONE

TYPICAL LANDSCAPE
Many species of conifer flourish in the dry climate and sandy soils of the Mediterranean. Wooded hillsides of conifers such as the distinctive Italian cypress, the tall maritime pine, or the distinctive stone pine are a familiar sight in this region.

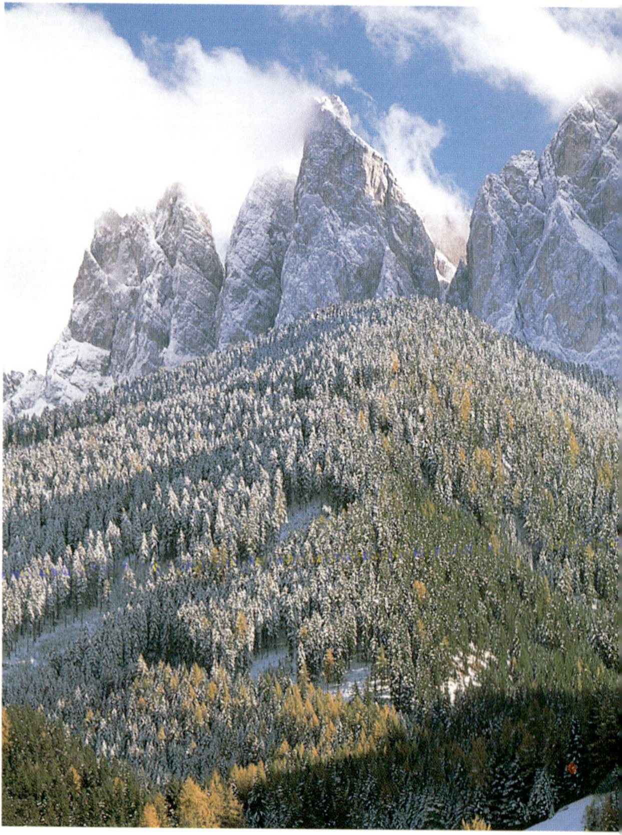

Mountain forests

The habitat 126
Rocky mountains 128
The himalayas 130

MOUNTAIN FORESTS

THE HABITAT

THERE ARE mountains on all of the continents. A few form great mountain ranges, such as the Rocky Mountains and the Himalayas. Mountain tops are always colder than the lowlands below, even in the tropics.

Alpine zone – alpine flowers, grasses, low vegetation

Subalpine zone – grasses and shrubs

Upper montane forest – conifers and a few hardy broadleaved trees

Lower montane forest – broadleaved trees and some conifers

Lowland vegetation

A HARSH CLIMATE
In mountainous areas, heavy snowfalls last from autumn until summer. On the highest peaks, snow lies frozen all year round.

MOUNTAIN SLOPES
Mountainside vegetation can be divided into zones. Lowland vegetation grows on the lowest slopes. Higher up, broadleaved trees give way to conifers. Above these are alpine meadows, then tundra.

HABITAT FACTS

- Mountain ranges are pushed upwards by the movement of the Earth's crust.
- The world's highest mountains are also the youngest – they have not yet been worn down by erosion.
- At the top of a mountain, high levels of ultraviolet light from the Sun stunt the growth of alpine plants.

THE HABITAT

TREE LINE AND LATITUDE

Himalayas 4000 m
Rocky Mountains 2000 m
Cairngorms 610 m
Sea level
70°N 57°N 47°N 30°N

LICHEN
Lichens are abundant on mountainsides. On the highest mountain slopes, tundra vegetation of lichens and mosses are often the only plants to be found growing there.

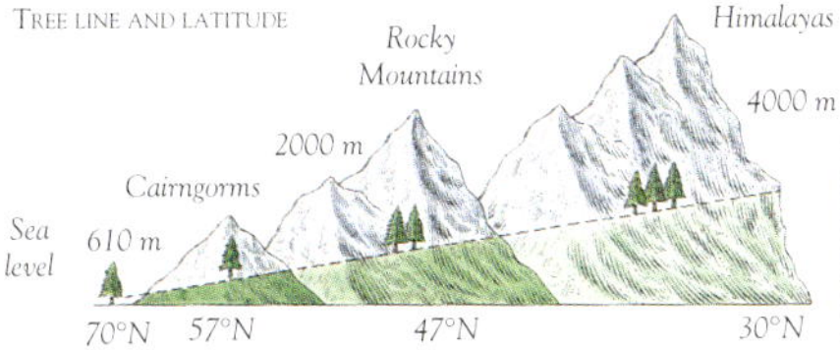

THE TREE LINE
Forests grow naturally on mountain slopes, but above a certain height, conditions become too harsh for trees to grow. This is called the tree line. The height of the tree line can vary, depending on how close the mountains are to the Equator. Only some conifers and a few hardy broadleaved trees can grow right up to the tree line.

DOLOMITES
Below the steep, snow-covered peaks of Southern Europe's Dolomite mountains grow conifers and broadleaved trees. Isolated mountain ranges are rather like islands. They often support species of plants and animals found nowhere else.

The mix of trees in the Dolomites is typical of an upper montane forest

127

MOUNTAIN FORESTS

ROCKY MOUNTAINS

THE ROCKY MOUNTAINS are the backbone of North America. They are made up of over sixty different mountain ranges, stretching from Alaska in the north, down through Canada and the United States, to Mexico in the south. Many of the trees here grow in national parks.

LODGEPOLE PINE
On mountain slopes, the lodgepole pine is a tall tree with a narrow crown and small cones. In coastal areas, it is a broad spreading tree with shorter needles and larger cones.

WESTERN YELLOW PINE
This fine pine grows on the eastern slopes of the Rockies. Native Americans used to gather flakes of bark to make hot, smokeless fires that would not give away their whereabouts.

JASPER NATIONAL PARK
This view shows Jasper National Park, Canada, in autumn. Dark, evergreen conifers contrast with the golden yellow of quaking aspens. This aspen is the most widespread North American tree.

ROCKY MOUNTAINS

Grey-green leaves striped underneath with two narrow white bands

MOOSE
The moose is the largest deer in the world. A male moose can weigh more than 450 kg (1,000 lb). It lives chiefly in the northern forests, but is also found farther south on the cool slopes of the Rockies. It eats the leaves and twigs of trees in the area.

SUBALPINE FIR
This conifer is characteristic of the Rocky Mountains, and grows up to the tree line. Its narrow crown is made of whorls of short, stiff branches that slope downwards. These may be covered in snow in winter.

These splashes of yellow are quaking aspen trees in autumn colour.

MOUNTAIN FORESTS

THE HIMALAYAS

THIS HUGE RANGE of mountains stretches from
Pakistan in the west to the far north-east of India.
The Himalayas contain some of the highest peaks
in the world, including Mount Everest, and support
a wide variety of unusual tree species.

Himalayan broadleaves

To the south of the Himalayas, tropical forests flourish on the
lower slopes. Higher up, flowering rhododendrons and magnolias,
brilliant displays of autumn leaves, and brightly coloured berries
illuminate the landscape.

TREE RHODODENDRON
This hardy rhododendron is
widespread across the Himalayas.
The large clusters of red
flowers show up in
contrast to the tough,
dark green leaves. The fruits
are small, woody
capsules that
contain tiny seeds.

Parallel veins along midrib

Flowers attract many insect pollinators.

Each flowerhead can contain up to 20 flowers

THE HIMALAYAS

Leaflets edged with fine teeth

Yellow patch turns red as flower ages

A CHEEKY BIRD
The white-cheeked bulbil is a common bird of the Himalayas, especially around settlements and villages. Attracted by scraps of food, these birds can become quite tame.

INDIAN HORSE CHESTNUT
This tree grows in the north-west Himalayas. It has smooth grey bark and leaves divided into five finely toothed, stalked leaflets. Each rough, scaly fruit contains one to three glossy, almost black seeds.

HIMALAYAN BIRCH
This birch is a true mountain tree that grows right up to the tree line, 4,000 m (13,000 ft) high. Below a thin, papery layer of peeling white, the bark is copper-coloured. Himalayan people use the bark for roofing.

131

MOUNTAIN FORESTS

Himalayan conifers

Above the tropical forests of the southern Himalayan slopes are mixed forests containing many fine coniferous trees. Some species, such as the deodar, produce high-quality timber that is in great demand. Other species are renowned for their bluish-green needles and gracefully shaped crowns. To the north of the Himalayas lies the stark, almost treeless plateau of Tibet.

HIMALAYAN PINE
Long, slender, bluish-green needles characterize this graceful tree. Its cones are 30 cm (12 in) long, and less woody than most pine

HIMALAYAN LANDSCAPE
This upland settlement is near Bemkar, on the slopes of the Himalayas. The houses are nestling among hardy conifer trees.

THE HIMALAYAS

BUDDHISM
Buddhism is one of the major religions of the world. Buddhists believe that the founder of the religion, Siddharta Gautama, was sitting under a tree when he received the ideas for his religion. This tree, the peepul tree, is now the sacred tree of India. It is also known as the bodhi, or enlightenment, tree.

Siddharta is also called Buddha

DROOPING JUNIPER
This juniper has drooping branches and small, aromatic cones with fleshy, blue-black scales. It grows best in sheltered valleys, but is a very hardy tree, surviving at altitudes of up to 3,600 m (12,000 ft), where it is often the only kind of tree.

WESTERN HIMALAYAN SPRUCE
This elegant spruce is found on the middle slopes of the Himalayas, between Afghanistan and Nepal. It is an attractive tree and is often planted as an ornamental. It has a narrow crown and drooping shoots. The cones have smooth, notched scales.

Pale-coloured shoots

Long, slender, curved leaves

Ripe cones are a glossy brown colour

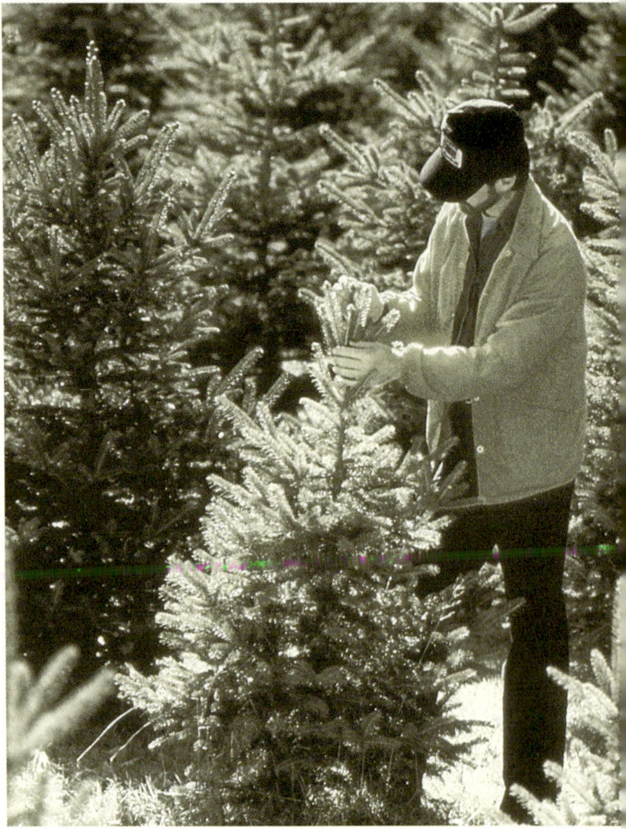

Reference Section

Studying trees 136
Watching trees grow 138
Threats to trees 140
Tree classification 142

REFERENCE SECTION

STUDYING TREES

ANYONE CAN STUDY TREES – it is an interesting and enjoyable hobby that you can do all year round. First get to know the trees in your neighbourhood. Some trees look bewilderingly similar at first, but as you become familiar with their shape, leaves, bark, flowers, or cones, you will be able to identify them with confidence.

TAKING NOTES
Make sketches and take notes to help you learn about the trees in your area. You will need a notebook, some pencils, and a magnifying glass.

LEAF SKELETONS
When a leaf falls from a tree, it begins to rot. The tiny veins that transport food and water around the leaf can be clearly seen in the remaining leaf "skeleton".

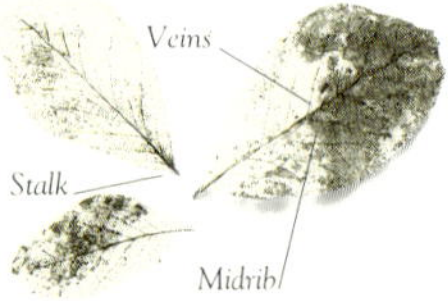

HOW TO MEASURE A TREE
Get a friend to stand under a tree. Hold a stick at arm's length so that the top lines up with your friend's head. Mark the stick in line with his or her feet. See how many times this measurement fits into the height of the tree. Multiply this number by your friend's height to calculate the tree's height

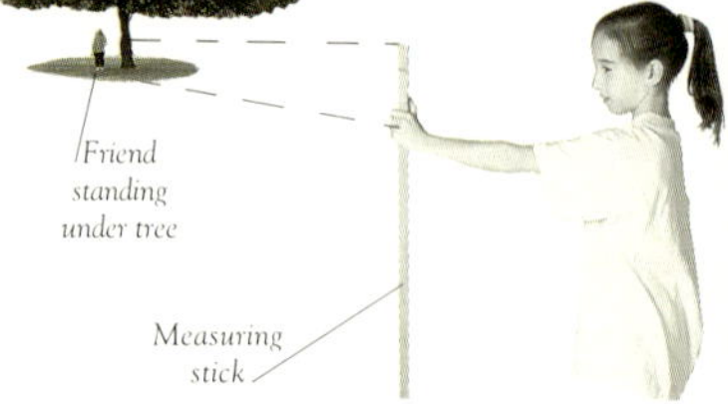

Veins

Stalk

Midrib

Friend standing under tree

Measuring stick

136

STUDYING TREES

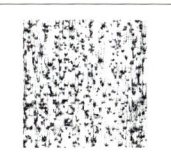

COMMON BEECH
This tree has a thin, fairly smooth bark. On the rubbing, this shows as a fine, mottled pattern.

ENGLISH OAK
The diamonds and ridges on this mature English oak show up well on this rubbing.

BARK RUBBINGS
You can compare the bark of different trees by doing bark rubbings. Pin or tape a piece of strong paper to the trunk. Using a wax crayon, rub lightly over the paper. Each kind of tree has its own pattern. Don't forget to make a note of the tree's name.

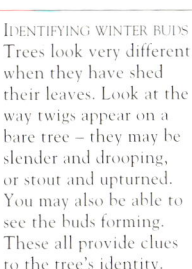

SCOTS PINE
Patchy, irregular flakes of bark characterize this conifer. They can be clearly seen here.

NORWAY SPRUCE
Mature Norway spruces have bark with small rounded plates, as seen on this rubbing.

IDENTIFYING WINTER BUDS
Trees look very different when they have shed their leaves. Look at the way twigs appear on a bare tree – they may be slender and drooping, or stout and upturned. You may also be able to see the buds forming. These all provide clues to the tree's identity.

ASH
Smooth, green-grey twigs with large black buds.

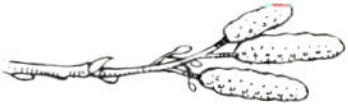

ALDER
Side buds grow on little stalks.

WHITE WILLOW
Slender twigs with buds wrapped in a single scale.

SWEET CHESTNUT
Stout, angular twigs with brownish buds.

REFERENCE SECTION

WATCHING TREES GROW

INSIDE EACH SEED there are the beginnings of a new tree, which will sprout and grow in the right conditions. You can try growing a tree from seed, and watch as it gets bigger every year. Some seeds take two months or longer to sprout, so be patient!

TWIGS IN WATER
In spring, if you cut two or three horse chestnut twigs and put them in a jar of water, you will be able to watch their buds open.

Hungry birds and insects are put off by the sticky gum.

Sticky bud scales protect the tightly furled new leaves.

Large scar left when last year's leaf fell in autumn

Whitish dots are lenticels, or pores, in the bark

FLOWERING BUD
As the sticky bud scales fall, the new leaves unfurl. At first, the leaves are pale and crumpled. As each leaflet expands, it turns darker green. If you look carefully into the centre of the bud, you will see a tiny spike of tightly closed flower buds.

WATCHING TREES GROW

Growing trees from seed

It is an exciting moment when your first seedling tree appears. You can collect ripe seeds from the ground in autumn. Remember to store them in a damp place until you are ready to plant them, as they will die if kept somewhere warm and dry.

You will need:

- Plastic bag
- Seeds
- Pebbles
- Spoon
- Soil
- Pot and saucer
- Bowl
- Watering can

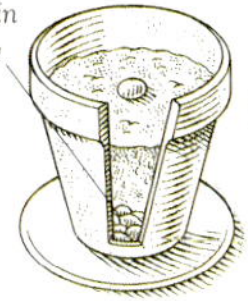

1 Soak the seeds overnight in water. As the seeds absorb the water, a tiny embryo starts to grow.

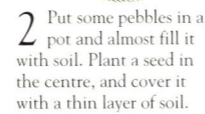

Pebbles allow water to drain away easily

2 Put some pebbles in a pot and almost fill it with soil. Plant a seed in the centre, and cover it with a thin layer of soil.

Fasten plastic bag with string or an elastic band

3 Tie a plastic bag over the pot to stop the soil drying out. Place the pot on a windowsill or in a greenhouse.

Tiny seedling tree

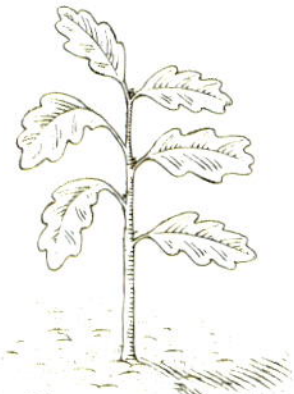

4 When the seedling appears, remove the bag and water the soil. Be careful not to over-water it or the seedling will rot.

5 Trees are not house-plants. Your seedling will do best outside during the summer, but remember to water it.

6 Plant your seedling in the ground in the autumn or the next spring. Make the hole a bit bigger than the pot.

THREATS TO TREES

FORESTS COVER ABOUT a third of the world's land surface, but many countries have only a tiny fraction of their original forests left. There are many reasons why forests have been cleared. Today, tropical forests are most threatened. Each year, over 5 million hectares (12 million acres) of rainforest are felled. At least 38 species tropical tree could become extinct.

LOGGING
Large numbers of trees are felled each year. Whole forests may be threatened if all the trees are logged. This also puts tribespeople and wildlife under pressure. If individual species with valuable timber are selected, this puts those species at risk.

FOREST FIRES
Fires are a natural part of some ecosystems, but to others they spell disaster. Fires started by humans often get out of control, damaging huge areas of forest. Tropical and temperate forests can be endangered by fire. It can take forests many years to recover.

FELLING
The chief reason for forest clearance is to obtain land for agriculture. Forests are also felled to build roads, houses, and settlements, or for mining operations. Many trees are felled for fuel.

HABITAT DESTRUCTION
Rare types of natural forest are threatened with destruction. These include tropical forests and ancient temperate forests. Island forests are particularly vulnerable, because they often contain species of tree found nowhere else in the world.

PESTS
Many pests that attack trees do only limited damage, but when alien pests, such as insects, fungi or even goats, are introduced to a forest, they can wreak havoc. Pests may be transported around the world deliberately or accidentally.

ACID RAIN
Acid rain is caused by industrial pollution. Oxides of sulphur and nitrogen are released by power station and factory chimneys. These dissolve in rain to form dilute acids that harm whole forests.

THREATS TO TREES

Endangered Forests

Name	Locality	Symbol
Conifer forest	N. America, N. and C. Europe, N. Asia	
Tropical forest	S. and C. America, Africa, S.E. Asia	
Temperate deciduous forest	N. America, Asia, Europe	
Mountain forest	Mexico, Andes, Himalayas	
Temperate evergreen forest	S. America, New Zealand, S.E. Australia	

Endangered Trees

Name	Locality	Symbol
3 species of Dipterocarpus	Sri Lanka	
3 species of pine (*Pinus*)	Mexico	
Brazilian rosewood (*Dalbergia nigra*)	Brazil	
Mahogany (*Swietenia macrophylla*)	Brazil, Peru, Guatemala	
Turraea decandra	Mauritius	
Tana river poplar (*Populus ilicifolia*)	Tanzania, Kenya	
Malapangit (*Tectona philippinensis*)	Philippines	

141

TREE CLASSIFICATION

THE PROCESS OF CLASSIFICATION arranges living things, plants and animals, according to features they have in common. Within plant classification, trees do not make up a single group, but are distributed throughout several families. Starting with the largest group, the plant kingdom, plants are divided up into increasingly narrow categories.

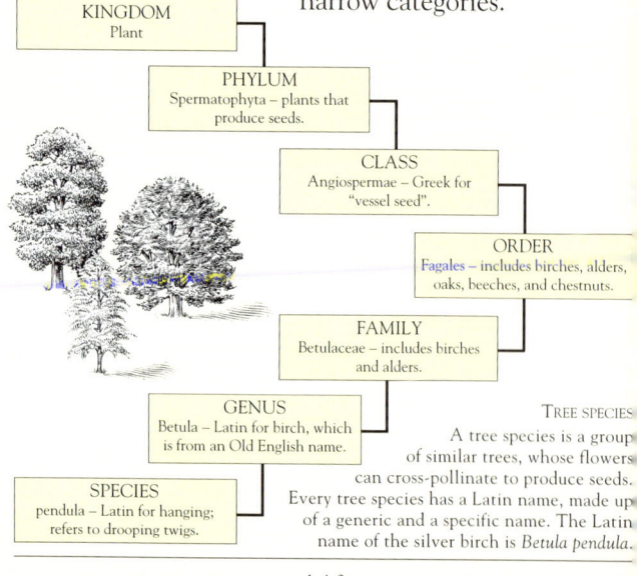

KINGDOM
Plant

PHYLUM
Spermatophyta – plants that produce seeds.

CLASS
Angiospermae – Greek for "vessel seed".

ORDER
Fagales – includes birches, alders, oaks, beeches, and chestnuts.

FAMILY
Betulaceae – includes birches and alders.

GENUS
Betula – Latin for birch, which is from an Old English name.

SPECIES
pendula – Latin for hanging; refers to drooping twigs.

TREE SPECIES
A tree species is a group of similar trees, whose flowers can cross-pollinate to produce seeds. Every tree species has a Latin name, made up of a generic and a specific name. The Latin name of the silver birch is *Betula pendula*.

TREE CLASSIFICATION

CLASS	SUBCLASS	ORDER	FAMILY AND SPECIES
GYMNOSPERMAE	CYCADATAE GINKGOATAE PINATAE	Cycadales	Cycadaceae – *Cycads*
		Ginkgoales	Ginkgoaceae – *Ginkgo*
		Taxales	Taxaceae – *Torreyas, Yews*
		Pinales	Araucariaceae – *Monkey Puzzle, Kauri*
			Podocarpaceae – *Podocarps*
			Cupressaceae – *Cypresses, Western Red Cedar*
			Taxodiaceae – *Redwoods*
			Pinaceae – *Pines, Spruces, Larches*
ANGIOSPERMAE	DICOTYLEDONEAE	Magnoliales	Magnoliaceae – *Magnolias, Tulip tree*
			Annonaceae – *Paw-paw*
		Laurales	Lauraceae – *Avocado, Cinnamon*
		Hamamelidales	Cercidiphyllaceae – *Katsura Tree*
			Platanaceae – *Planes, Buttonwood*
			Hamamelidaceae – *Witch hazel, Sweet gum*
		Myricales	Myricaceae – *Wax Myrtles*

REFERENCE SECTION

Class	Subclass	Order	Family and Species
ANGIOSPERMAE	DICOTYLEDONEAE	Fagales	Betulaceae – *Alders, Birches*
			Fagaceae – *Beeches, Chestnuts, Oaks*
		Casuarinales	Casuarinaceae – *She Oak, River Oak*
		Caryophyllales	Phytolaccaceae – *Ombu*
		Theales	Theaceae – *Camellias*
			Dipterocarpaceae – *Keruing, Merantis*
			Guttiferae – *Mangosteen*
		Malvales	Tiliaceae – *Limes, Basswoods*
			Sterculiaceae – *Bottle Tree, Cacao*
			Bombaceae – *Balsa, Baobab, Kapok*
		Urticales	Ulmaceae – *Elms*
			Moraceae – *Figs, Mulberries*
		Lecythidales	Lecythidaceae – *Brazil nuts, Cannonball Tree*
		Violales	Caricaceae – *Papayas*
			Tamaricaceae – *Tamarisks*
		Salicales	Salicaceae – *Poplars, Willows*
		Capparales	Moringaceae – *Horseradish Tree*
		Ericales	Ericaceae – *Madrona,*

TREE CLASSIFICATION

Class	Subclass	Order	Family and Species
ANGIOSPERMAE	DICOTYLEDONEAE		*Strawberry Tree*, *Rhododendron*
		Ebenales	Sapotaceae – *Chicle*, *Gutta-percha*, *Sapodilla*
			Ebenaceae – *Ebonies*, *Persimmons*
			Styracaceae – *Snowbell Trees*, *Silverbells*
		Rosales	Pittosporaceae – *Lemonwood*
			Eucryphiaceae – *Eucryphias*
			Rosaceae – *Apples*, *Stone fruits (Plums etc)*, *Rowans*, *Hawthorns*
		Fabales	Leguminosae- *Acacias*, *Judas Tree*, *Laburnums*, *Locusts*, *Tualang*
		Myrtales	Lythraceae – *Cape Myrtles*
			Rhizophoraceae – *Mangroves*
			Myrtaceae – *Eucalypts*
			Combretaceae – *Indian Almond*
		Cornales	Nyssacaceae – *Tupelos*, *Handkerchief Tree*
			Cornaceae – *Dogwoods*
		Proteales	Proteaceae – *Silky Oaks*, *Macadamia*
		Santalales	Santalaceae –

REFERENCE SECTION

Class	Subclass	Order	Family and Species
ANGIOSPERMAE	DICOTYLEDONEAE	Celastrales	Sandalwoods Celastraceae- *Spindle Trees, Maytenus* Aquifoliaceae – *Hollies, Yerba-maté*
		Euphorbiales	Euphorbiaceae – *Rubber Trees, Manchineel, Umbrella Tree*
		Rhamnales	Rhamnaceae – *Buckthorns*
		Sapindales	Sapindaceae – *Soapberries, Litchee* Hippocastanaceae – *Horse Chestnut, Buckeyes* Aceraceae – *Maples, Box Elder* Burseraceae – *Gumbo Limbo* Anacardiaceae – *Mango, Pistachio* Simaroubaceae – *Tree of Heaven* Meliaceae – *Mahoganies* Rutaceae – *Citruses* Zygophyllaceae – *Lignum Vitae*
		Juglandales	Juglandaceae – *Hickories, Pecan*

TREE CLASSIFICATION

Class	Subclass	Order	Family and Species
ANGIOSPERMAE	DICOTYLEDONEAE	Geraniales	Erythroxylaceae – *Coca Tree*
		Umbellales	Araliaceae – *Devil's Walking Stick*
		Gentianales	Loganiaceae – *Buddlejas*
			Apocynaceae – *Devil Tree Frangipani*
			Oleaceae – *Ashes, Olives, Lilac*
		Polemoniales	Ehretiaceae – *Cordias*
		Lamiales	Verbenaceae – *Teak*
		Scrophulariales	Bignoniaceae – *Indian Bean Tree, Calabash*
		Rubiales	Rubiaceae – *Cinchonas, Coffee Trees*
		Dipsacales	Caprifoliaceae – *Elders*
	MONOCOTYLEDONEAE	Pandanales	Pandanaceae – *Screw Pines*
		Arecales	Palmae – *Palms*
		Liliales	Agavaceae – *Joshua Tree, Dragon Tree*

Glossary

ALTERNATE
Leaves that are arranged along a stem in two rows, but not opposite each other.

ANGIOSPERM
A plant with flowers, and with seeds that are enclosed inside a fruit.

ANTHER
Sacs at the tip of the stamen, where pollen is produced.

BARK
The tough protective layer that covers the trunk, branches and twigs of a tree.

BIPINNATE
Leaves that are divided into leaflets, which are divided yet again into even smaller leaflets.

BRACT
A scale-like leaf at the base of a flower or flowerhead that often protects the buds.

BROADLEAVED TREE
A tree that has flowers, and seeds with two cotyledons.

BUD
A compact shoot made up of an immature stem, leaves, or flowers, which are all encased in protective scales.

CALYX
The outer, protective layer of a flower bud, made up of sepals.

CAMBIUM
The actively growing layer between xylem and phloem that makes a tree trunk become a little thicker every year.

CAPSULE
A dry kind of fruit that opens at special slits or pores to release its seeds.

CARPEL
The female reproductive parts of a flower, which consist of the ovary, style, and stigma.

CATKIN
A hanging flowerhead of small, single-sexed flowers arranged along a central stem.

CELLULOSE
The substance from which plant cell walls are made.

CHLOROPHYLL
The green pigment that absorbs the energy in sunlight to make food by photosynthesis.

COMPOUND LEAF
A leaf that is divided into leaflets.

CONE
The male or female reproductive structures of most gymnosperms.

CONIFER
A cone-bearing tree.

COTYLEDONS
Simple leaves that develop inside a seed and usually store food for the growing embryo.

GLOSSARY

CUTICLE
A waterproof, waxy layer that covers the outer surface of leaves.

DECIDUOUS
A tree that sheds all its leaves during the autumn in temperate regions, or at the beginning of the dry season in the tropics.

DROUGHT
A long period of time without rainfall.

DUCT
A small tube.

ENDOCARP
The innermost layer of the fruit wall.

EMBRYO
In a seed, the very tiny plantlet that develops after pollination.

ENTIRE
A leaf whose margin is not cut into teeth or lobes.

EPICARP
The outermost layer of the fruit wall.

EQUATOR
An imaginary line around the Earth, halfway between the North Pole and the South Pole.

EVERGREEN
A tree that sheds and renews its leaves all the time, so that the tree is never without leaves

FILAMENT
The fine, thread-like stem of a stamen that connects the anther to the rest of the flower.

FRUIT
The part of a flower that completely encloses its developing seeds.

GERMINATION
The beginning of embryo growth and development.

GYMNOSPERM
A flowerless plant whose seeds are not enclosed within a fruit.

HARDY
Able to survive in a cold climate.

HEARTWOOD
Non-living wood that makes up the centre of a tree trunk and that provides mechanical support only.

INFLORESCENCE
A flowerhead.

LAMINA
The blade of a leaf.

LEAFLET
Each part of a compound leaf.

LENTICEL
A tiny pore in the bark of the trunk or roots, which is filled with loosely packed cells that allow gases to pass into or out of the bark.

LIGNIN
A substance that reinforces cells to make them woody and rigid.

LOBED
A leaf that is divided into parts that are not completely separated into leaflets.

REFERENCE SECTION

MANGROVE TREE
A group of trees that grow in tropical coastal swamps.

MEDULLARY RAY
A thin, vertical sheet of living cells in the woody tree trunk that stores and transports food materials across the trunk.

MESOCARP
The middle layer of the fruit wall.

MIDRIB
The central vein of a leaf blade.

MINERAL NUTRIENTS
Chemicals dissolved in soil moisture that are vital to the growth of a plant.

NATIVE
A plant or animal that occurs naturally in a particular place.

NECTAR
A sugary liquid produced by flowers to attract insect and animal pollinators.

OPPOSITE
Two rows of leaves that grow along a stem in pairs opposite each other.

OVARY
The part of the carpel that contains the female sex cells of the plant.

PALMATE
A leaf divided into lobes, or leaflets that radiate like the fingers of a hand.

PERICARP
The whole fruit wall.

PETAL
Part of a flower, usually coloured or scented to attract pollinators.

PETIOLE
The stalk of a leaf.

PHLOEM
Tubes that carry dissolved sugars around the tree.

PHOTOSYNTHESIS
The process by which green plants harness the energy in sunlight to make sugars from carbon dioxide and water. This process is carried out in the presence of the green pigment chlorophyll.

PIGMENT
A coloured substance.

POLLARDED
A tree that has had its branches trimmed back to the top of its trunk.

POLLEN
The male sex cells of a seed bearing plant.

POLLINATION
The process during which pollen from the stamens is deposited on the stigmatic surface of a plant in the same species.

RECEPTACLE
The tip of a flower stalk, which is situated just below the flower.

RELICT
The last remnants of a group of trees that were once widespread and abundant.

150

GLOSSARY

Resin
A sticky, aromatic substance that oozes from wounds, mostly from coniferous trees, and helps to prevent decay and insect attack.

Root hairs
Minute projections of the cells at the end of rootlets, which absorb water and dissolved minerals.

Sapwood
The band of non-living wood that surrounds the heartwood, and conducts water.

Savannah
Areas of natural or semi-natural tropical grassland, usually with brief rainy periods and scattered trees.

Seed
The reproductive unit of gymnosperm and angiosperm plants.

Sepal
A part of the calyx, which envelops and protects the flower bud.

Simple leaf
A leaf that is not divided into leaflets.

Stamen
The male reproductive part of a flower, which consists of filament and anthers, or pollen sacs.

Stigma
The part of the carpel upon which pollen lands.

Stomata
Pores, found mostly on the undersurface of leaves, which open to allow gases to enter and leave the leaf, and close to prevent the loss of excess water vapour.

Style
The part of the carpel that connects the stigma to the ovary.

Temperate
The band of the Earth between the hot tropics and the cold polar zones.

Tepal
The term used for sepals and petals that appear identical.

Testa
The outer layer of a seed.

Toothed
A leaf with a serrated edge.

Tropical
The band of the Earth between the Tropic of Cancer and the Tropic of Capricorn that has a warm climate.

Tropic of Cancer
The imaginary line that circles the Earth at latitude 23 deg 27 minutes North.

Tropic of Capricorn
The imaginary line that circles the Earth at latitude 23 deg 27 minutes South.

Vein
In a leaf, the strand of conducting tissue which is made up of xylem and phloem.

Xylem
Tubes of non-living cells that carry water from the roots to all other parts of a plant.

Latin name index

Amur cork tree (*Phellodendron amurense*), 12 m (40 ft) Dec

Apple (*Malus domestica*), 10 m (33 ft) Dec

Atlas cedar (*Cedrus atlantica*), 40 m (130 ft) Ev

Austrian pine (*Pinus nigra*), 40 m (130 ft) Ev

Banyan (*Ficus benghalensis*), 25 m (80 ft) Ev

Baobab (*Adansonia digitata*), 23 m (75 ft) Dec

Basswood (*Tilia americana*), 23 m (75 ft) Dec

Bay laurel (*Laurus nobilis*), 15 m (50 ft) Ev

Bird cherry (*Prunus padus*), 15 m (50 ft) Dec

Black beech (*Nothofagus solandri*), 25 m (82 ft) Ev

Black locust (*Robinia pseudoacacia*), 40m (130 ft) Dec

Black poplar (*Populus nigra*), 30 m (100 ft) Dec

Black spruce (*Picea mariana*), 30 m (100 ft) Ev

Black walnut (*Juglans nigra*), 24 m (80 ft) Dec

Brazil nut (*Bertholletia excelsa*), 45 m (148 ft), Dec

Bristlecone pine (*Pinus aristata*), 15 m (50 ft) Ev

Bull bay (*Magnolia grandiflora*), 25 m (82 ft) Ev

Bunya pine (*Araucaria bidwillii*), 35 m (115 ft) Ev

Californian buckeye (*Aesculus californica*), 10 m (33 ft) Dec

Californian laurel (*Umbellularia californica*), 30 m (100 ft) Ev

Candelabra tree (*Euphorbia ingens*), 9 m (30 ft) Ev

Carapa guianensis, 40 m (130 ft) Dec

Caucasian wingnut (*Pterocarya fraxinifolia*), 30 m (100 ft) Dec

Cedar of Lebanon (*Cedrus libani*), 40 m (130 ft) Ev

Chinese plum yew (*Cephalotaxus fortunei*), 9 m (30 ft) Ev

Chinese wingnut (*Pterocarya stenoptera*), 25 m (82 ft) Dec

Chusan palm (*Trachycarpus fortunei*), 10 m (33 ft) Ev

Cider gum (*Eucalyptus gunnii*), 25 m (80 ft) Ev

Cinnamon (*Cinnamomum zeylanicum*), 12 m (40 ft) Ev

Cocoa (*Theobroma cacao*), 15 m (50 ft) Ev

Coconut (*Cocos nucifera*), 30 m (100 ft) Ev

Coffee (*Coffea spp*), 3 m (10 ft) Ev

Common alder (*Alnus glutinosa*), 25 m (82 ft) Dec

Common beech (*Fagus sylvatica*), 35 m (115 ft) Dec

Common fig (*Ficus carica*), 9 m (30 ft) Dec

Common / English oak (*Quercus robur*), 30 m (100 ft) Dec

Cork oak (*Quercus suber*), 28 m (90 ft) Ev

Date palm (*Phoenix dactylifera*), 20 m (66 ft) Ev

Dawn redwood (*Metasequoia glyptostroboides*), 40 m (130 ft) Dec

Dogwood (*Cornus florida*), 12m (40 ft) Dec

Douglas fir (*Pseudotsuga menziesii*), 60 m (197 ft) Ev

Drooping juniper (*Juniperus recurva*), 15 m (50 ft) Ev

English elm (*Ulmus procera*), 30 m (100 ft) Dec

European ash (*Fraxinus excelsior*), 40 m (130 ft) Dec

Forrest's fir (*Abies forrestii*), 20 m (66 ft) Ev

Ghost gum (*Eucalyptus papuana*), 15 m (50 ft) Ev

Hawthorn (*Crataegus*

monogyna), 10 m (33 ft) Dec
Himalayan birch (*Betula utilis*), 25 m (82 ft) Dec
Himalayan pine (*Pinus wallichiana*), 40 m (130 ft) Ev
Hinoki cypress (*Chamaecyparis obtusa*), 40 m (130 ft) Ev
Holly (*Ilex aquilifolia*), 20 m (66 ft) Ev
Holm oak (*Quercus ilex*), 30 m (100 ft) Ev
Horse chestnut (*Aesculus hippocastanum*), 30 m (100 ft) Dec
Hungarian oak (*Quercus frainetto*), 30 m (100 ft) Dec

Incense cedar (*Calocedrus decurrens*), 40 m (130 ft) Ev
Indian bean tree (*Catalpa bignonioides*), 15 m (50 ft) Dec
Indian horse chestnut (*Aesculus indicus*), 30 m (100 ft) Dec
Italian cypress (*Cupressus sempervirens*), 50 m (164 ft) Ev

Japanese cedar (*Cryptomeria japonica*), 45 m (148 ft) Ev
Japanese cherry (*Prunus serrulata 'Kanzan'*), 10 m (33 ft) Dec
Japanese maple (*Acer palmatum*), 10 m (33 ft) Dec
Judas tree (*Cercis siliquastrum*), 10 m (33 ft) Dec

Kapok tree (*Ceiba pentandra*), 55 m (180 ft) Dec
Katsura tree (*Cercidiphyllum japonicum*), 30 m (100 ft) Dec
Kauri (*Agathis australis*), 45 m (148 ft) Ev
Keaki (*Zelkova serrata*), 40 m (130 ft) Dec
Korean pine (*Pinus koraiensis*), 35 m (115 ft) Ev
Kowhai (*Sophora microphylla*), 10 m (33 ft) Dec

Laburnum (*Laburnum anagyroides*), 7 m (23 ft) Dec
Larch (*Larix sp.*), 40 m (130 ft) Dec
Lemon (*Citrus limon*), 7 m (23 ft) Ev
Lodgepole pine (*Pinus contorta var. latifolia*), 25 m (82 ft) Ev

Madrona (*Arbutus menziesii*), 40 m (130 ft) Ev
Magnolia dawsoniana, 12 m (40 ft) Dec
Magnolia delavayi, 10 m (33 ft) Dec
Maidenhair tree (*Ginkgo biloba*), 40 m (130 ft) Dec
Monkey puzzle (*Araucaria araucana*), 30 m (100 ft) Ev
Monterey cypress (*Cupressus macrocarpa*), 25 m (82 ft) Ev
Monterey pine (*Pinus radiata*), 30 m (100 ft) Ev
Mountain ash (*Eucalyptus regnans*), 60 m (197 ft) Ev

Mountain ribbonwoood (*Hoheria glabrata*), 10m (33 ft) Dec

Norway maple (*Acer platanoides*), 25 m (80 ft) Dec
Norway spruce (*Picea abies*), 50 m (164 ft) Ev

Oriental plane (*Platanus orientalis*), 30 m (100 ft) Dec
Oil palm (*Elaeis guineense*), 30 m (98 ft) Ev
Olive (*Olea europea*), 15 m (50 ft) Ev

Paper birch (*Betula papyrifera*), 30 m (100 ft) Dec
Patagonian cypress (*Fitzroya cupressoides*), 50 m (164 ft) Ev
Pawpaw (*Carica papaya*), 8 m (26 ft) Ev
Peach (*Prunus persica*), 8 m (26 ft) Dec
Pear (*Pyrus communis*), 15 m (50 ft) Dec
Peepul (*Ficus religiosa*), 25 m (80 ft) Ev
Pistacia (*Pistacia vera*), 10 m (33 ft) Dec
Plum (*Prunus domestica*), 10 m (33 ft) Dec
Pyrus calleryana, 15 m (50 ft) Dec

Redbud (*Cercis canadensis*),

10 m (33 ft) Dec
Red maple (*Acer rubrum*), 25 m (82 ft) Dec
River birch (*Betula nigra*), 30 m (100 ft) Dec

Scots pine (*Pinus sylvestris*), 35 m (115 ft) Ev
Shagbark hickory (*Carya ovata*), 23 m (75 ft) Dec
Silver birch (*Betula pendula*), 18 m (59 ft) Dec
Silver fir (*Abies alba*), 40 m (130 ft) Ev
Silver wattle (*Acacia dealbata*), 20 m (66 ft) Ev
Sitka spruce (*Picea sitchensis*), 50 m (164 ft) Ev
Southern beech (*Nothofagus sp.*),
Stone pine (*Pinus pinea*), 20 m (66 ft) Ev
Strangler fig (*Ficus destruens*), 30 m (100 ft) Ev
Strawberry tree (*Arbutus unedo*), 10 m (33 ft) Ev
Sugar maple (*Acer saccharum*), 30 m (100 ft) Dec
Sugar pine (*Pinus lambertiana*), 70 m (230 ft) Ev
Summit cedar (*Arthrotaxis laxifolia*), 10 m (33 ft) Ev
Swamp cypress (*Taxodium distichum*), 40 m (130 ft) Dec
Sweet chestnut (*Castanea sativa*), 30 m (100 ft) Dec
Sweet gum (*Liquidambar styraciflua*), 40 m (130 ft) Dec
Sweet orange (*Citrus sinensis*), 10 m (30 ft) Ev
Sycamore (*Acer pseudoplatanus*), 30 m (100 ft) Dec

Tamarind (*Tamarindus indica*), 25 m (82 ft) Ev
Tree mallow (*Hibiscus syriacus*), 3 m (10 ft) Dec
Tree rhododendron (*Rhododendron arboreum*), 15 m (50 ft) Ev
Tualang (*Koompassia excelsa*), 75 m (246 ft) Dec
Tulip tree (*Liriodendron tulipifera*), 50 m (164 ft) Dec
Tupelo (*Nyssa sylvatica*), 25 m (82 ft) Dec
Turkish hazel (*Corylus colurna*), 25 m (82 ft) Dec

Ulmo (*Eucryphia cordifolia*), 40 m (130 ft) Ev

Veitch's fir (*Abies veitchii*), 25 m (80 ft) Ev

Water tupelo (*Nyssa aquatica*), 30 m (100 ft) Dec
Wellingtonia (*Sequoiadendron giganteum*), 80 m (262 ft) Ev
Western hemlock (*Tsuga heterophylla*), 60 m (197 ft) Ev
Western Himalayan spruce (*Picea smithiana*), 40 m (130 ft) Ev
Western red cedar (*Thuja plicata*), 50 m (164 ft) Ev
Western yellow pine (*Pinus ponderosa*), 50 m (164 ft) Ev
Whistling thorn (*Acacia drepanolobium*), 10 m (30 ft) Dec
White cypress (*Chamaecyparis thyoides*), 25 m (82 ft) Ev
White oak (*Quercus alba*), 35 m (115 ft) Dec
White poplar (*Populus alba*), 30 m (100 ft) Dec
Willow (*Salix sp.*), Dec

Yezo spruce (*Picea jezoensis*), 50 m (164 ft) Ev

Index

A
acacia tree, 13, 101, 106
acorn, 42, 67
Africa, tropical forests, 100-1
alder, 69, 137
Alocasia thibautania, 103
alternate leaves, 22, 148
Amur cork, 82
Andes Mountains, 97, 118
angiosperm, 14, 148
anther, 33, 148
apple tree, 33, 35, 81
ash tree, 15, 29, 52, 137
Asia, tropical forests, 102-3
aspen, 128-9
Atlas cedar, 122, 123
Australia:
 mixed evergreen forests, 112-3
 tropical forests, 106-7
Australian mountain ash, 15
Austrian pine, 25

B
Balkans, 76-7
banyan trees, 103
baobab, 101
bark, 20, 28-9, 148
 rubbings, 137
bark beetle, 28
basswood, 63
bay tree, 120
beech tree, 14, 44-5, 66, 75, 137
bipinnate leaves, 148
birch tree, 30, 53, 66, 68, 131

bird cherry, 14
black beech, 115
black locust, 65
black poplar, 75
black spruce, 53
black walnut, 65
bonsai, 20, 89
boreal forest, 50
bracket fungi, 26
bract, 32, 37, 148
Brazilian rosewood, 141
bristlecone pine, 16
broadleaved trees, 12, 14-5, 148
 Himalayas, 130-1
 Japan, 88-9
 leaves, 22-3
 mixed evergreen forest, 108-23
 pollination, 40
buds, 148
 apical, 39
 conifers, 24
 flower, 32
 winter, 22, 137
bull bay, 64
bunya pine, 107

C
cactus, 13
California, 116-7
Californian buckeye, 33
Californian laurel, 116
calyx, 148
cambium, 27, 28, 39, 148
Cameron Highlands, 104

candelabra tree, 101
canopy:
 temperate forests, 60
 tropical forests, 94, 96
capsules, 148
Carapa guianensis, 97
carbon dioxide, 39
carob tree, 120
carpels, 32, 33, 148
catkins, 33, 148
 alder, 69
 black poplar, 75
 Chinese wing-nut, 84
 hazel, 40, 79
Caucasian wingnut, 78
cedar of Lebanon, 79
cedars, 24, 36, 90, 112, 117, 122, 123
cells, 26, 38, 39
cellulose, 26, 148
Central America:
 tropical forests, 96-7
Central Europe:
 temperate forests, 74-5
chestnut:
 horse, 76, 131, 138
 sweet, 35, 137
China:
 temperate forests, 82-7
Chinese plum yew, 17, 25
Chinese wing-nut, 84
chlorophyll, 23, 39, 148
cider gum, 113
citrus fruits, 34, 80
cloud forests, 104-5
compound leaves, 23, 148

155

cones, 16, 17, 36-7, 148
conifers, 12, 16-7, 148
  Himalayan, 132-3
  Japanese, 90-1
  leaves, 24-5
  pollination, 40
  relict, 84
conkers, 76
cork, 82, 121
cotyledons, 34, 44-5, 148
crab apple, 41
crown, 20-1
cuticle, 22, 25, 149
cypresses, 16, 24, 70-1, 117, 119, 122, 123

D
date palm, 18
dawn redwood, 84
deciduous trees, 12, 14, 60, 149
deodar, 132
Dipterocarpus, 141
dogwood, flowering, 32
douglas fir, 37
drooping juniper, 133

E
elm, English, 60
embryo, 34, 44, 149
emergents, 94
endangered forests, 140-1
endocarp, 34, 149
English oak, 13, 67, 137
epicarp, 34, 149
eucalyptus trees, 106, 107, 112-3
Europe:
  coniferous forests, 50
  temperate forests, 60, 66-7, 74-7

F
fig, common, 42
filament, 33, 149
fir trees, 17, 24, 37, 74, 91, 129
flower bud, 39
flowers, 20, 32-3, 34, 40-1
fly agaric, 30
forests:
  coniferous, 47, 48-57, 141
  endangered, 140-1
  mixed evergreen, 47, 108-23, 141
  mountain, 46, 126-33
  temperate, 46, 58-91, 141
  tropical, 47, 92-107, 141
fruits, 20, 149
  cultivated, 80-1
  dispersal, 42-3
  growth, 34-5
  riverside trees, 68
fungi, 26, 30, 140

G
germination, 44-5, 149
ghost gums, 106
ground beetles, 51
growing trees, 138-9
growth, 38-9
growth rings, 27
gymnosperms, 16, 149

H
hawthorn, 43, 72, 73
hazel, 40, 79
heartwood, 27, 149

hedge, 72-3
hickory tree, 62
Himalayan birch, 131
Himalayan pine, 132
Himalayas, 126, 130-3
Hinoki cypress, 24-5
holly, 14, 73
holm oak, 110
horse chestnut, 76, 131, 138
humus, 61
Hungarian oak, 77

I
incense cedar, 117
Indian bean tree, 68
Indian horse chestnut, 131
inflorescence, 33, 149
insect pests, 140
insect pollination, 32, 41
Italian cypress, 123
ivy, 26

J
Japanese cedar, 90
Japanese maple, 88
Judas tree, 78
jungles *see* tropical forests
juniper, 133

K
kapok, 96
katsura tree, 88
kauri, 110, 114
keaki, 85
Korean pine, 82
kowhai, 111

L
laburnum, 43

156

lamina, 23, 24, 149
larch, 24, 25, 52
laurel, 88, 116
leaflet, 23, 149
leaves, 20
　broadleaved trees, 14, 22-3
　conifers, 24-5
　seed, 34, 44-5
　skeletons, 136
lenticels, 29, 149
Lepidodendron, 12
lichen, 50, 127
lignin, 26, 39, 149
liverwort, 97, 105, 115
lobed leaves, 23, 149
lodgepole pine, 128
logging, 57, 140

M
madrona, 116
magnolia, 33, 87, 130
mahogany, 141
maidenhair tree, 24, 85
mangrove tree, 30, 149
maple, 23, 63, 88
Maritime pine, 123
Mediterranean: mixed
　evergreen forests, 120-3
medullary ray, 27, 150
mesocarp, 34, 150
midrib, 22, 150
minerals, 30, 38, 41, 150
mist forests, 104-5
monkey puzzle tree, 118
monsoon forests, 94
montane forest, 97, 102, 104-5, 126
Monterey cypress, 117
Monterey pine, 16

moss, 26, 50, 56, 97, 105, 111, 115, 127
mountain ash, 15, 113
mountain forests, 46, 126-33, 141
mountain ribbonwood, 115

N
nectar, 41, 150
needles, pine, 24, 51
New Zealand, 114-5
North America:
　coniferous forests, 56-7
　mixed evergreen forests, 116-7
　mountain forests, 128-9
　temperate forests, 60, 62-5, 70-1
Norway maple, 23
Norway spruce, 16, 17, 24, 50, 137
nutrients, 38, 61, 68
nuts, 35, 42, 80-1, 98

O
oak trees, 26, 61
　acorns, 15, 42, 67
　common, 13, 67, 137
　cork, 121
　holm, 110
　Hungarian, 77
　seedlings, 44
　white, 23, 62
oil palm, 98
olive tree, 121
opposite leaves, 22, 150
ovary, 33, 150
ovules, 40
oxygen, 30, 39

P
Pacific forests, 56-7
palm trees, 12, 18-9
palmate leaves, 150
paper, 54-5
paper birch, 53
Patagonian cypress, 119
peepul tree, 102, 133
pericarp, 150
pests, 140
petals, 32, 34, 41, 150
petioles, 23, 150
phloem, 38, 150
photosynthesis, 39, 45, 50, 150
pine trees, 30, 110, 122
　bristlecone, 16
　Himalayan, 132
　Korean, 82
　lodgepole, 128
　Monterey, 16
　needles, 24, 51
　Scots, 40
　stone, 123
plane trees, 23, 76
plantations, 54, 98
pneumatophores, 30
pollen, 40
pollination, 32, 36, 40-1, 150
poplar, 75, 77, 141
Prunus serrulata "Kanzan", 89

Q
quaking aspen, 128-9
quarter sawing, 55

R
rainforests:
　bark, 29

157

New Zealand, 115
see also tropical forests
receptacle, 35, 150
red maple, 63
redbud tree, 32
redwood, 24, 39, 84
resin, 24, 28, 29, 65
river birch, 68
riverside trees, 68-9
Rocky Mountains, 126, 128-9
root hairs, 30, 38, 150-1
roots, 20, 30-1

S
Saguaro cactus, 13
saplings, 60
sapwood, 27, 151
savannah, 100-1, 106, 151
scale leaves, 24
Scots pine, 40, 51, 137
seed leaves, 34, 44-5
seedlings, 44-5, 139
seeds, 32, 34-5, 151
 broadleaved trees, 14
 conifers, 16, 36
 dispersal, 42-3
 germination, 44-5
sepals, 32, 151
shagbark hickory, 62
shrub, 12, 72-3
silver birch, 66
silver fir, 17, 74
silver wattle, 113
simple leaves, 23, 151
sitka spruce, 56
South America:
 mixed evergreen forests, 118-9
 tropical forests, 96-7
southern beeches, 111, 112, 114, 118
spruces:
 black, 52, 53
 Norway, 50
 sitka, 56
 western Himalayan, 133
 white, 52
 Yezo, 83
stamen, 32, 33, 151
stigma, 33, 151
stomata, 22, 151
stone pines, 123
strawberry tree, 120
style, 33, 151
subalpine fir, 129
sugar maple, 63
sugar pine, 37
summit cedar, 112
swamp cypress, 30, 71
swamp tupelo, 70
sweet chestnut, 35, 137
sweet gum, 65
sycamore, 35

T
taiga, 50
tamarind pods, 34
Tana river poplar, 141
temperate forests, 46, 58-91, 141, 151
tepals, 33, 151
testa, 34, 151
toothed leaves, 151
tree line, 46, 127
tree mallow, 39
tree rhododendron, 130
tropical forest, 47, 92-107, 141, 151
trunk, 20, 26-7
tualang, 102
tulip tree, 41
tupelo, 14, 70
Turkish hazel, 79

U
ulmo, 119

V
veins, 14, 22-3, 136, 151
Veitch's fir, 91

W
walnut tree, 55, 65
water tupelo, 70
weeping willow, 87
wellingtonia, 16, 27
western hemlock, 51, 56
western Himalayan spruce, 133
western red cedar, 36, 57
western yellow pine, 128
wetlands, 70-1
whistling thorn acacia, 101
white cypress, 70
white oak, 23, 62
white poplar, 77
white willow, 137
wind pollination, 40
winter buds, 22, 137

X
xylem, 38, 151

Y
yew, 24
Yezo spruce, 83

158